THAT IS THAT

Essays About True Nature

THAT IS THAT

Essays About True Nature

NIRMALA

Endless Satsang Foundation

Endless Satsang Foundation

www.endless-satsang.com

CONTENTS

PART 1

Being in the Present Moment

WHAT IS THIS MOMENT'S TREASURE?

What is this moment's treasure? There is so much happening right now as you read these words. Thoughts, feelings, desires, sensations, and the whole world of objects and events are all taking place in this very moment. And yet, we often look outside this moment for happiness, satisfaction, freedom, and even our true nature. When you look outside of what is actually happening, all you can ever find is an idea or a fantasy. That's what not being in the present moment means, not that you are actually somewhere else, but that you are *looking* somewhere else. The only other place to look is in your own mind, at a story about another time, or even a story about the present moment.

The tricky thing is that our stories are very convincing. The mind is a good storyteller. And every now and then, one of our stories comes true: The thing we were imagining actually happens, although never exactly as we imagined it. And if we are honest, we have to admit that this is quite rare. However, any psychology student will tell you that an intermittent reward is more powerful as a reinforcement than even a constant reward. We are so powerfully rewarded when a story our mind tells comes true that we simply overlook the many times our stories turn out to be irrelevant.

Where is there a more constant reward? What can we pay attention to that is accurate and true? One thing we can say about our present moment experience is that it's always accurate and true. We don't have to wonder if it's going to come true or not, since it already has! So the content of our present moment experience is always true. Even the thoughts we are having in the present moment are truly thoughts. It is undeniably true that we are thinking whatever we are thinking, even if the content of the thought is not true. So every experience we are having right now is a true experience. It has some reality and significance, unlike the content of our thoughts, which may or may not have significance.

If our present moment experience is always real and true, why do we pay so little attention to it? Why aren't we filled with wonder and curiosity about this endless parade of true, real experiences showing up in every moment? That fact that we aren't fascinated by what's happening in the present moment isn't due to any lack in the present moment but to the simple misunderstanding that we think that what matters is what happens, when what makes a moment satisfying and worthwhile is the *awareness* of what happens.

If our focus is completely on what is happening, then there's always something better that could be happening instead. And since our minds are good at telling us what could or should be happening instead, we tend to focus on what could or should be happening. If what matters is what happens, then it makes sense to pay attention to what we want to happen, or at least to what we don't want to happen in hopes that we can prevent it from happening. If what's important is the content of our experience and, by extension, the content of our thoughts, then of course we'll pay attention to the content of our thoughts.

But what if the most important thing is what is aware of what is happening? What if what really matters is both the nature of awareness and the specific quality of our awareness in this moment? This is the nine-hundred pound gorilla in the room that nobody is talking about. The awareness of the present moment is a constant feature of every moment. This awareness is a complete mystery, and yet it is the source of all the joy, peace, happiness, satisfaction, and love we have ever had. It may seem like satisfaction and happiness come from what is happening, but satisfaction and happiness come from the flow of awareness to whatever is happening.

Recognizing this fundamental truth about the source of joy, peace, and love can dramatically simplify your life. It turns out that it doesn't matter that much what is happening. The real treasure in this moment is always to be found in the awareness of this moment, not in the content of our experience. So it's not that important if something better is happening or not. Discovering this simple perspective is like discovering you live in a candy store: Everywhere you turn is another goodie!

Beyond that, is the recognition that this endless supply of goodies is what you really are. You are not the content of your experience; you are the awareness that brings life and joy to every experience. Talk about not having to worry about what happens! Nothing that happens can change what you are, and what you are is the biggest treasure. It is hidden in plain sight, right in front of you, always in the experience you are having right now.

TWO POSSIBILITIES

In every moment, there are two possibilities. One possibility is to have all of our curiosity, attention, and passion focused on what is happening. The other is to have that same curiosity, attention, and passion focused on what is *not* happening, what is *not* present, or what we think should or shouldn't be happening. In every moment, the question is: What are you giving your attention to? Are you allowing what *is* or going to battle with it, trying to change it in some way?

When our focus is on what is, our experience of what is opens up and becomes bigger, richer, and more complete. But when it is on what is *not* (the past, the future, or any thought about what is), our experience of the moment contracts and becomes narrower and full of suffering and struggle, because inherent in a focus on what is *not* is a struggle with what *is*.

When we look, we discover that most of the time we are in opposition to what is and oriented toward what is not. Life is mostly about how to make things better and get more pleasure or how to get rid of things that are painful. We are constantly evaluating our experience, looking to see what's wrong with it and how it could be improved. We tend to be focused on what's wrong with the moment or on what could be added to it to make it better. As a result, our attention becomes very narrow and our awareness limited.

Once we see how much time we spend struggling with what is, the tendency is to go to battle with that—to try to fix that tendency to try to change everything. But that only changes the content of our struggle: Now we are struggling with our tendency to try to change things. We suffer over the fact that we are suffering.

The other possibility is to just notice how much you suffer, without trying to do anything about it. Just allow the fact that you don't allow much. Just recognize that that is the way it is. This struggling with what is, is just what we were conditioned to do, and this conditioning is also a part of what is.

Once we stop being in opposition to what is, it is possible to see how all our struggling comes from the idea of a *me*. Without the assumption that something is *my* experience, there wouldn't be much point in trying to change anything about the moment. Our effort and struggle to change what is only makes sense if there is a me. It is all in service to maintaining the idea of a me. In fact, the struggle *is* the me. When there is no struggle, there is no me. All of our suffering is the result of having and maintaining an identity.

Once we realize this, the tendency is to try to fix this—to try to change our belief about who we are. We focus on getting rid of identification, which is focusing on what is not again. We are still suffering because we are at war with our tendency to identify. Instead of accepting what is (our tendency to identify), we are oriented toward how we think it should be: I should know better than to be caught in identification. I should know who I really am.

Another possibility is to be really present to this tendency to identify without making any effort to change it. If that's what is happening, then that's what is happening. You just let it be that way. You can even be amazed by it all, including the fact that there is a sense of a me. You see how unreal this me is, but you don't struggle to be rid of it. There's no longer an assumption that something is wrong that needs to be fixed.

When it's finally okay for the moment to be just the way it is— including the fact that we identify with a me and therefore battle with the moment—then more of our experience can be recognized and included in our awareness. If we are willing to be present to and allow our identification and whatever else is happening, then it's also possible to notice something beyond identification, something beyond our struggle and effort to maintain a me. What that something is, for lack of a better word, is Being.

Along with awareness of identification and the struggle and suffering inherent in that, is an awareness of the larger ground of Being in which everything is happening. When we see that all the me is and ever has been is a lie, but we don't turn away from that awareness or judge ourselves for it or try to get rid of the me, then we can notice that, along with the struggling inherent in the me, there is a beautiful, rich Presence, or Being, that is allowing everything, including the experience of me. We come to see that the me's struggle is only a tiny percentage of our entire experience and that this struggle is happening in an ocean of allowing. This allowing is Being.

When we are allowing, we include in our awareness what it is that is allowing, and that is Being, which is who we really are. This realization can be a jolting experience or a quiet one, since Being is actually very familiar. Every moment of allowing has actually been a moment of experiencing Being.

THE MIND'S ENDLESS TO-DO LIST

The mind has a tendency to label everything as bad or a problem. If we wake up stiff in the morning, the mind calls that bad and then worries about getting older. If we find out we are being let go at our job, the mind immediately assumes the worst and worries about the future. Even if something good happens, the mind sees the possible downside or worries about losing what it has just gained.

The mind sees its job as rejecting what is presently going on in order to bring about a better future. Its logic is that if we are happy now, we won't do anything to make things better. So it looks for what's wrong with the way things are so that it can figure out what to do to fix or improve things. This keeps the mind very busy and leaves us with an ongoing sense of incompleteness and lack. Because there is always something going on that could be labeled bad, there is always something to fix or improve upon. As a result, we have an ever-expanding to-do list in our minds. We may feel the need to improve our diet, our appearance, our finances, our health, our relationships, our career. More immediately, we may feel the need to change how we feel whenever a strong feeling or sensation occurs.

We even have to-do lists for being better spiritually: I need to be more aware or present. I need to be less judgmental. I need to find my life purpose. I need to be more intuitive. I need to be more compassionate. I need to have a deeper experience of Oneness. Spiritual teachings are mostly descriptions of our true nature and affirm that we already are what we are seeking, and yet spiritual seekers often turn such teachings into prescriptions for how to achieve a better reality. Spiritual seekers aren't necessarily looking for the truth, but for a more spiritual to-do list. Even when told that awareness is all there is and life is already loving and perfect, they want a list of steps to take to feel that way more often.

There is a simple question that can short circuit this tendency to feel we need to fix this moment or improve upon it: Is this moment really so bad? Is there really anything present right now that is a problem? What if stiffness in the morning isn't bad but just a particular sensation? What if feeling stiff is actually okay? We can ask the same question about anything we are experiencing: Is sadness a bad sensation? Is confusion a bad sensation? Is the lack of money really a problem in this moment? Is the loss of a job or a relationship really a problem in this moment? In this moment, there is never really a problem, only ideas or stories about a problem.

This kind of questioning does the opposite of adding to our to-do list. Instead, it can reduce the sense of having to do something about what is happening right now. Even if something still needs to be done about whatever is happening, questioning our mind's conclusions can put the need to do something in perspective and reduce the sense of overwhelm created by the endless litany of problems the mind can imagine and the ever-growing list of things we think we need to do about them.

More importantly, inquiring into what is true about this very moment can put us in touch with the beauty and wonder that is always present in this mystery called life. Not only is there nothing problematic or bad in the here and now, but there is also a limitless amount of depth and richness to be found in the present moment. Everything that really matters, such as peace, joy, satisfaction, connectedness, and love, is found in the here and now, and only in the here and now. To experience this fullness and wonder, there's nothing we need to do except question the conclusion that peace, joy, satisfaction, and love are not already here and then look to see if they are. Is any peace present right now? Is there any love at all in this moment? What is that peace like? What is the nature of the love that is here now? Asking these kinds of questions is all it takes to get in touch with the amazing richness of the present moment. And there is nothing we need "to do" about it.

A SEA OF SENSATION

Without looking to the mind for an answer, can you just notice what is here right now? Does the sea of sensation, energy, and Presence that is here right now really make up something called a body or a person? Or does it make up a sea of sensation, energy, and Presence? We are used to letting the mind tell us what is so, just as we get used to having the news on television tell us what's happening. But when it comes to our own experience, we can go directly to the source.

What is the sensation in your arms right now? Can you put it into words, or is it something beyond words? And what about the space around your arms? Does your sensing really stop where your skin stops, or is there some kind of impression of the entire area around your arms right now? Where is the awareness that senses your arms located? Is it in your head, or is it in your head and your arms?

Questions like these aren't meant to lead you anywhere except where you already are. When every experience, including the most ordinary, is so mysterious, there is no need for a profound experience of bliss or cosmic light. If you happen to have an experience of bliss, then you can explore that. But for now, why not explore what is already here?

The wonderful thing about this simple form of inquiry is that you are never done inquiring. A new sea of sensation, energy, and Presence is unfolding in each moment's experience. Even thoughts and feelings are just a flow of internal sensations: voices, pictures, and emotional energies that ebb and flow. How do you know what you are sensing right now? How do you know what you are thinking or feeling right now? What is it that registers all the movement, color, sound, pressure, texture, language, contrast, and space that is happening right now as you read these words?

There is a wonderful relief in asking these questions and not having to formulate an answer in your mind. The questions are an invitation to fully taste and savor the exquisite flavors of life. Life doesn't need a conclusion to be alive.

THE CAUSE OF SUFFERING

Being alive in a human form is often experienced as difficult. We struggle and suffer and rarely feel all right with the world and ourselves. What is this sense of difficulty? What causes this sense of difficulty and pain? What is the source of our suffering? What does it mean to suffer?

Every moment is full of a symphony of sensations, thoughts, and feelings. Take a moment just to experience how much is happening right now: sounds, sights, tactile sensations, smells, internal sensations, thoughts, feelings, pressure, desire or longing. It's impossible to compile a list of everything you are experiencing in this moment because there's so much. And all of it is constantly changing into a new set of sensations, thoughts, and feelings.

Along with the raw sensations and random thoughts filling the moment, is often an internal reaction to whatever we are experiencing. Most of the time, we are internally busy with a rejection of or attempt to manage the experience we're having. This internal activity is effortful and involves a tensing and pushing against something we're experiencing either externally or internally. This internal efforting is the true source of all our pain and suffering.

This is good news, since it means that no experience or sensation by itself can cause us to suffer. We have to resist it or struggle with it for it to become painful. If we simply allow ourselves to be fully aware of the experience or sensation we are having without struggling against it, the suffering or pain is gone.

THE GAP IN AWARENESS

We usually think that suffering is caused by bad experiences, but it's actually caused by our attention flowing toward something that isn't here, toward something that isn't very true, such as an idea or a fantasy, which are very small truths. Suffering ends when our attention is flowing toward what's actually happening, what's true in the moment. Suffering is the distance—the gap—between what we are oriented toward and what is. However large the gap is between what is actually happening and what you are putting your attention on is how much you will suffer. If there's no gap, then there's no suffering.

That gap can be present regardless of whether something good or bad is happening. For example, if someone you love is dying, your awareness may be so fully focused on what's happening in that moment that the experience lacks the suffering you would expect, although suffering may appear later if thoughts creep in about how things should or could have been. In contrast, there are times when things are going really well and you're suffering, often because you're afraid of things changing. If this truth is understood—that your happiness doesn't depend on what is happening—it can change your life. It may not affect what's happening, but it will change your experience of it.

Our hopes, dreams, desires, fears, doubts, and worries aren't really happening, so they are very small truths. When we give our attention to something that isn't actually happening, we suffer. When our attention is focused on these things, we never feel satisfied because they don't nourish us. But when we give our passion and curiosity to more of what's true in the moment, we don't suffer. What are you giving your awareness, your passion, your curiosity to?

It's very simple: Our suffering is a matter of how much of our attention is flowing toward what isn't actually present, such as hopes, dreams, desires, fears, doubts, worries, ideals, and fantasies. What we are desiring isn't present or we wouldn't be desiring it. Nor is what we fear. Our fears are just as much of a figment of our imaginations as our desires. None of these thoughts are real, and giving our attention to what is unreal brings us out of contact with what is real, where the aliveness of Being can be experienced.

Rejection and desire are the mechanisms with which we resist what is, which results in our suffering. They operate in a cycle: We go back and forth from rejection to desire. We think, "This isn't good. Maybe if I got this or if I meditated more or if I had a better lover or more money or more freedom, it would be better." Then we go about trying to fulfill that desire and, regardless of whether we succeed or not, we come back to the point where we still reject whatever is present now. Even when we get what we think we want, we may find that it's not that great, so we dream up something else we believe will make things better.

This activity of desiring what isn't present and rejecting what is creates and sustains the sense of a small self—the me. If things are lousy, they're lousy for whom? For *me*. And if things could be better, better for whom? Better for *me*. We're often not even conscious of rejecting and desiring because we're caught up in the content of our desires and fantasies. We get so hypnotized by our fantasies that we aren't even aware they are contracting our sense of self and making us feel very small, incomplete, deficient, and unsatisfied.

Nevertheless, that sense of incompleteness can be trusted. It's telling you how true it is that your fantasy will make you feel better. The sense of incompleteness and smallness in the experience of fantasizing shows you just how little truth there is in your fantasy.

Fantasies aren't very true. They only exist in our mind. There isn't much substance or reality to them. You can also trust when your Heart feels very full and complete. The simple alternative to rejection and desire is to give your attention to all of what is here right now, not just to your thoughts and feelings.

The biggest surprise is discovering that there is no suffering even in our suffering! When you give all of your attention to the actual experience of rejection and desire, the suffering inherent in it dissolves. When we become curious and attentive to the process of rejection, it no longer has any sting. If you become fully present to the movement of thought, a thought can be recognized for what it really is: just a thought!

THE SUFFERING IN THE WORLD

Q: *The world we live in is becoming an ever-increasing source of distress and pain. What can we do? Must we suffer these things?*

A: I do believe it's possible for the world situation to be transformed, and I also believe it's possible to transcend suffering. Just by letting things be the way they are, suffering dissolves (suffering was never real to begin with). Letting things be the way they are is also the most likely condition under which transformation on all levels can occur. Letting things be isn't the cause of change, but rather it creates conditions that allow our deeper intelligence to work. You ask what you can do. The answer is to simply allow everything to be the way it is and also be as curious and present to it all as you can. It is this mix of acceptance and curiosity that allows the open flow of our divine intelligence and inspiration to move in the world. There's no nice, neat formula to what this looks like, and so any transformation or healing of our distress and difficulties will unfold organically and probably in a completely surprising and unexpected way.

***

A friend emailed and reported that even in the midst of a profound experience of Oneness, she is still saddened by the suffering in the world, and she wonders why consciousness seems to need to suffer so much. Here is my response:

The question of why consciousness needs suffering is a difficult question to answer, but we can get a hint of the answer by noticing how much suffering opens our Heart. It seems that even though consciousness is infinite, it still likes to stretch itself by opening even wider. Eventually we as individuals learn that we don't need to suffer to open the Heart. It is a great relief to realize that we can just go directly to the love and the softness. But until we learn this, life keeps reminding us to open our Heart even wider by showing us the suffering that arises when we don't.

Even when we have surrendered and given our Heart totally to the truth, we still experience the suffering of others so that we are inspired to reach out and show them the same love that has rescued us. The pain itself is a good hurt like the good hurt from exercise. In the end, suffering was all just an idea of suffering, and what is really happening is this stretching and unfolding of our infinite Heart. There's no suffering in the depths of love, and there never has been.

SENSING INSIDE

We often look into our mind to know something. So when we want to know ourselves, we often look into the mind for that also. But the mind is full of thoughts *about* what we want to know and never the thing itself. You will never find an apple or a lover or a sunset or anything in your mind, just thoughts about these things. And you will never find your true Self in the mind, just a lot of thoughts about the true Self. That is just what the mind is made of and so that is what you find in there.

What if you sense in your heart instead? I am not suggesting you think about what you might find in your heart. What if you actually sense the space inside your chest? What is actually here right now within the space of your body? It can be helpful to rest your hands over your chest, and then simply notice what is really present beneath your hands. No need to think much about it, just directly sense what's here.

First of all, how mysterious is it that there is a body with a heart? And even more mysterious is the simple existence of space beneath the hands resting on your heart. What is this simple mystery of a place called here? Why is there a "here" that holds your body and everything else that is present? What is that space itself under your hands like? If, for just a moment, you don't think about what's here and instead just sense the actual space under your hands, what do you find?

And even if right now you feel relatively little or even nothing in the space of your heart, what is that "nothing" like? What are the qualities of the space itself? Is it light or heavy, bright or dark, clear or foggy? And if there are specific sensations present in the space of your Heart, what are those like? What does it mean that there are sensations here inside of you? How is it possible to be sensing them? What is sensing them?

These questions aren't meant to get you thinking about the mystery of your body, the space your body is in, or the awareness that senses the body and space. These questions are simply an invitation to experience all of it just as it is right now. Your thoughts will never satisfy your curiosity about your true nature, but this direct sensing can show you more than you ever imagined about it.

NOTICING GRATITUDE

Gratitude is often suggested as a well meaning prescription. We are told to express gratitude and to be grateful for what we have. And yet it's difficult to feel something you are told to feel, even if it would feel better than what you are feeling. But what if gratitude is a description of your deeper nature? What if deep within, you already feel gratitude?

Awareness—Being—is full of gratitude. Awareness loves the sensations, experiences, and thought forms that it touches in each moment. There is a natural appreciation for all that exists in awareness itself. Awareness can't help itself, because on the deepest level awareness recognizes everything it touches as its own self. There is only awareness, and that is what awareness experiences in every moment, and that is what it is grateful for.

And yet, that is not our conscious experience in many, if not most, moments. It seems like much of what awareness touches isn't something we appreciate or are grateful for. What about our problems and painful experiences? Suggesting that we be grateful for those things can seem ridiculous when we are in the midst of rejecting them.

The key to aligning with the deeper level of our being where gratitude flows so freely is very simple. It only requires that you notice the gratitude you do feel in this very moment. Notice what awareness is actually touching in this very moment, as that is where the gratitude is rising to the surface of awareness.

Another trick to accessing the deeper level of our being where gratitude flows is, when you find yourself rejecting something, just notice, or admit, how much you are enjoying rejecting it. Although you may not feel grateful for something when you're rejecting it, you still may be able to feel gratitude for your own judgment and discrimination in rejecting it. You may also find that when you let yourself feel gratitude for your ability to reject something, you end up feeling some gratitude for what you are rejecting. It's okay to feel gratitude for all of it!

Fundamentally, awareness just loves experience of all sorts. So even if you are unable to get past your upset to the actual reality of this moment, then awareness just enjoys the upset. Every emotion and sensation is richly unique, and awareness is deeply grateful for every experience that comes.

PART 2

Making Up Reality

GOING NAKED WITHOUT BELIEF

Something means what we decide it means. This whole life is make-believe: We make up our beliefs and then believe them. We make it all up as we go, and each moment we are also free to make up a new story. We are free to decide what this means and what that means and also free to change our mind and decide the opposite is true. So when you think enlightenment is important, then it is important. When you think enlightenment is meaningless, then it is meaningless. When you think what you do is useless, then it is useless. When you think you must go through an ego death, then it will seem like you have to go through an ego death.

I'm not saying that you decide what happens. I'm saying that when something happens, you decide what it means. Meaning is like a work of art that we paint with our thoughts and that we are constantly retouching and recreating. This doesn't mean that things have no meaning, unless you decide they have no meaning; it just means that the meaning something has is the meaning we give it.

Given the fluid, ever-changing nature of thought and therefore of meaning, the best approach is to believe whatever you believe but hold it lightly. We need a certain structure of belief to function and orient in the world. But we don't need a final belief or formula for how something works or what something means. You can play with beliefs and meanings and see what effect they have. If a belief is working—great. And if a belief isn't working—great, because then you can change it.

In the midst of all of this exploration of beliefs, it is also fine to take a break and just not believe. I'm not suggesting you decide that things have no meaning, but that you take a break from knowing what things mean or wondering if something has meaning. Not knowing is only a problem if you think it matters what you think. If you have a sense of how such thoughts are make-believe, then it will feel okay to go naked for a while with no belief. Then if you want to believe something for a change, put on some belief clothing again.

When you allow yourself to not know, there is the possibility of seeing things as they really are. And even then, it's fine to make up a story and make believe it's true and see reality that way. The ultimate isn't a complete and permanent cessation of knowing, but the flexibility to know or not know from moment to moment. This includes the flexibility to experience the depths of pure Being without the filter of knowing, and it also includes every knowing, belief, or meaning you have ever experienced. This flexibility of knowing isn't a prescription or something you achieve, but a description of your consciousness as it is now and as it has always been.

Everything you have ever experienced has been an expression of this capacity you have to make believe. There is no right thing to experience, and there is no wrong thing to experience. Life is showing you the full range of your consciousness, from constricted, narrow beliefs to the boundless dimensions of reality, unfiltered by meaning or beliefs. It is the dance between these two—reality and belief—that makes up your experience in every moment. You might as well enjoy the show!

THE DANCE BETWEEN THE MIND AND REALITY

Q: *It is true that our beliefs change over time. Sometimes even in one day we may think two different things about reality and how everything functions. But then is there anything objective? Is there any final truth, or is everything subjective? What is reality like outside our minds and beliefs? Do we create our worlds with our beliefs and mind?*

A: There are several perspectives on the question of what is objectively real, and they all have some truth to them. One perspective is that the only thing that is truly real is what doesn't come and go or what is eternal. According to this definition, nothing with a form or name is real. The only thing that is real is the mystery beyond name and form, which is the source of everything. This is a very absolute perspective, and it can be very powerful in dissolving worldly attachments. It cuts through all appearances to the infinite, empty Presence at the core of all existence.

Another perspective suggests that everything is real, that there is ultimately just one thing here, and it is very real. Everything is a part of this reality, so everything is real and everything is connected. This is a more heart-centered perception, and it can be very powerful in opening up the qualities of love, compassion, and acceptance inherent in our true nature.

A third possibility is a kind of combination of the first two: realizing that there is just one thing, and so everything is real, and at the same time, being able to discriminate how much reality there is in any experience. Some things have a lot of reality, and some things have very little. For instance, a thought or belief has some reality but not very much. All of your thoughts fit between your ears, so how big can they actually be? This third perspective is a more practical and functional approach that evokes our capacity for discrimination and effective action.

These three perspectives are summed up in the famous quote by Nisargadatta: "When I see I am nothing, that is wisdom. When I see I am everything, that is love. My life is a movement between these two." All three perspectives are true, and they all have a place in a complete understanding of reality. Yet none of them contain the whole truth, which is an inherent limitation of words and ideas.

To answer your question, I would suggest that there is objective reality and also subjective reality, and life is a dance between these two. Reality outside of the mind and beliefs is pure, empty, limitless potential. That is the biggest truth, and yet it isn't a final truth, since life apparently doesn't stay as pure potential, but loves to move through mind and beliefs into form. Life is purely objective in its resting state as eternal, infinite space; and it can become purely subjective when it moves into the realm of thoughts that have no correspondence to outer reality, like when we are daydreaming about a perfect lover. Most of the time reality or experience is a mixture of objective reality and subjective reality.

The more objective our experience is, the more substantial, lasting, and profound it is; and the more subjective our experience is, the more temporary and unsubstantial it becomes. Neither one is better or worse, but they are definitely different experiences, and we can discriminate how real or true each experience is. Since our minds are the source of subjective reality, the mind isn't very useful in discriminating how real something is. To the mind, everything looks equally real, so the mind isn't very helpful in distinguishing between objective and subjective reality. Fortunately, we also have a Heart, which is naturally able to distinguish how real or true an experience is. Truth or reality opens the Heart and quiets the mind. In contrast, something that isn't very true or real contracts the Heart and makes the mind busier.

This dance between objective reality and subjective beliefs is very alive and dynamic. Our experience can change dramatically in even a single day or moment, with every thought or idea that pops into our head, and even more dramatically, when there is little or no thought, and an aspect of objective reality shines through. So experientially, there would appear to be no final experience of truth, but instead an endless unfolding play of truth with itself. What an amazing dance life creates!

As to whether we create our reality with our subjective thoughts and beliefs, I would suggest we co-create our subjective reality along with all of the other consciousnesses here. Our thoughts and beliefs have an effect on how reality appears, which is how this dance of life works: Everything affects everything else. So even our thoughts in their limited subjective existence have an effect on everything else that happens. However, there's still the question of how much effect they have. Do our thoughts create the entire reality we experience? Or is reality also affected by other people's thoughts? And is human thought the only player in this game? What if there are many levels of Being that all have a part in this dance? What about our collective thoughts or beliefs? What about the thoughts or beliefs arising in the mind of God? What if there are an infinite number of conscious forces at work shaping objective reality into subjective experience?

So the answer may be that our beliefs affect reality along with everything else that affects reality. It could be that ultimately the creation of our reality is the sum total of everything that affects the unfolding of life, which includes our personal thoughts and beliefs. This can put in perspective how important what we think and believe is—it may not matter that much in the creation of reality.

You can play with the effect that your beliefs have without taking them too seriously. It turns out that most of what happens is the result of much bigger forces that we might call destiny or grace.

MAKE BELIEVE

We are by nature belief-making creatures. Just like squirrels hide their nuts, humans make up beliefs. It is how we create the meaning in our life and how we organize and define the story of our life. Each of us is the novelist or screenwriter for the story of me, and we do this by making believe that what we think about our life is the whole truth.

However, it is possible to realize that while this process of defining our reality is very creative, challenging, and even fun, it is never complete or fully accurate. Our beliefs leave out a lot of the reality of a situation. For instance, if we believe someone is a nice person, we have left out that person's shadow side. If we believe that someone is a jerk, we have left out some of the good things about him or her. The limited nature of belief applies to not only our beliefs about others, but also our beliefs about ourselves. We have an identity that is composed of our beliefs about ourselves, and that identity is therefore as fluid, changeable, and incomplete as any other set of beliefs.

This is not a problem and is even a very creative process. However, we often forget we are making something up: We make believe we are a good person or better than others and then forget that this is at best only half of the truth. It's like watching a movie, forgetting it's fictional, and then feeling upset by the actions of the characters for hours or days after the movie has ended. The actors were paid to behave badly, but we've forgotten that it was all made up.

So, while there's nothing wrong with our beliefs and identities, they can cause us to suffer when we forget that we make them up. If we hold them rigidly and defend them from any contradiction, they can limit our awareness and actions. We are stuck in a make-believe movie created by our own mind, and we forget that we can change the script anytime. Knowing that reality is not as you believe it is, doesn't necessarily mean you change anything about your experience. But knowing that can allow you to enjoy the experience as it is, just as knowing that you are watching a movie can allow you to enjoy the outrageous antics of a superhero or the desperate acts of a heart-broken lover without becoming too upset. Forgetting that your interpretations of your own life are just as made up can mean that, instead of enjoying the richness of every experience, you are busy trying to change things in order to solve the problems that your own beliefs have created.

What does it mean that you are broke or wealthy? What are you like when someone has made you the butt of a joke? How do you feel when your career soars or crashes? Who do you think you really are? You get to make up the answers to all of these questions and millions more. And in the midst of this incredibly creative storytelling about your existence, there is also the opportunity to look beyond the story to see what else is here. What is present right now that isn't part of your beliefs? What is the real reality underlying your make-believe reality? What creates the physical world? What creates the mind that is creating your beliefs? There's no need to reach definitive answers to these questions, as that would just be another belief. Instead, you can play with endless new answers to every question and thereby discover the limitless potential of your true nature. Make believe is fun!

THOUGHTS ARE NOT VERY REAL

Our beliefs, stories, ideas, fears, hopes, wishes, desires, projections, and wounding are just thoughts. Thoughts exist and therefore have some reality and some effect on reality, but they don't have very much reality. When we become contracted, it's because we're involved with a story in our mind. Interestingly, we can become just as contracted when we are involved with a positive story, such as, "I'll win the lottery, find the perfect lover, live in a big mansion, and become enlightened." If you check when an elaborate story like that is happening, you'll find that your awareness and sense of self in that moment is actually very contracted, very small, which reflects how little truth such thoughts have.

Contraction isn't bad or wrong, it's just different from and not as pleasant as not being contracted. Imaginary things like our fears, projections, hopes, and dreams can only be experienced when our awareness is contracted. Our awareness must contract to fit into the small reality of our imagined experience. The antidote isn't to get rid of thoughts and fantasies (we can't anyway), but to see them for what they really are: small truths. A small truth isn't bad or worse than a bigger truth, just as a shoebox isn't worse than a garage—it's just smaller. But it's good to be able to tell the difference between a shoebox and a garage so that you don't try to store your car in a shoebox or build a garage to store a pair of shoes! In discriminating how big something is, you naturally recognize its appropriate usefulness. Thoughts are useful when they refer to something that's real, but all by themselves, thoughts—especially fears—have little function. To focus exclusively on your fears or hopes doesn't usually serve much purpose.

There is much more going on in every moment than our thoughts about the future or the past, our fears, doubts, beliefs, dreams, desires, judgments, and opinions. The bigger truth is the experience of love, joy, and peace to be found here and now in your true nature. Why leave out what's real and true? You don't have to get rid of your fears, desires, judgments, or other thoughts, but why make them more important than they are? What if they are actually quite small, and your strength, wisdom, joy, love, and awareness are limitless? When you put your fears and other thoughts into perspective, they no longer have much capacity to make you suffer, even if they continue to arise in your mind.

THE GHOSTS WITHIN

Most of us think of a ghost as something that only exists after we die, which continues to hang around and haunt the places we lived while alive. What if there are ghosts of yourself that are around while you are alive? What if what you think you are is actually a ghost?

As we usually think of them, ghosts are insubstantial forms that come and go. They aren't solid or real, and most people can't see them. And yet, how substantial or real are our images of ourselves, our ideas about who we are? If you have an image of yourself as an attractive person one day and an unattractive person the next day, how real is either image? And can other people see your self-image? What does it mean if you have a self-image of being unattractive and someone is attracted to you anyway? Maybe they can't see your self-image. Maybe your self-image is a kind of ghost. We aren't always willing to see that our idea of ourselves is a kind of ghost because we really believe that our self-image is what we are.

We may wonder, "Who am I if what I think I am is something insubstantial and not real? What is here besides the ghosts of my self-images?" There's a sense that we do exist, that we are real. But does this sense of existence and reality come from our image of ourselves or from something else, something deeper within our being? It's difficult to know for sure, since the self-image and the sense of realness can be present simultaneously, and our egoic idea of ourselves can co-opt that deeper sense of realness.

One measure of how real something is how long it lasts. The more real something is, the longer it lasts. How long do ideas about yourself last? They come and go (like a ghost in a ghost story) and don't last very long at all. A thought is often over so quickly that we can't even remember it a moment later. Images of ourselves are constantly changing and fading away, to be replaced by other images or thoughts about something else. So those images or identities must not be very real. They may just be ghosts in our minds.

What about the pure sense that you exist right now? Does that come and go? How often do you have the opposite sense—that you don't exist at all? The sense that you exist is more real than your ideas about yourself because it doesn't come and go. You exist, but your ideas about yourself are just ghosts. What you are isn't contained in your ideas or identities. What you really are is still here even when your ideas about yourself fade away, like ghostly images in a movie.

What matters is the real you. You can become more curious about this real you than you are about the false ghosts of identity. What is the real you made of? What is it like? What does it want? What can it do? These are rich and meaningful questions to explore, but remember that the real answers aren't found in your ideas about yourself, but only in the simple sense that you exist.

NOT KNOWING

We spend much of our life in pursuit of knowledge. It seems you can never know too much, and our families and culture all support this approach to life. As a result, most of us find it uncomfortable or even frightening to not know something. It seems difficult to not know what to do, what you want, or what is going to happen.

But what if there is a richness and possibility in the experience of not knowing? What if, in our rush to get to a place of knowing and certainty, we pass over the empty spaces of uncertainty that may contain even deeper truths? Life is complex and has many dimensions. The more subtle and profound elements of life don't easily fit into concepts and ideas—our usual type of knowing. Discovering these deeper dimensions may require a slowing down in our thought and action to allow the quieter and deeper aspects of existence to be recognized. Is not knowing really a place of lack or incompleteness, or is there something worthwhile to be found in the silent moments when we don't know anything?

There's nothing wrong with knowing something when you do know it. But it turns out there is also nothing wrong with not knowing, and not knowing can even lead to surprising new depths of knowing. Becoming familiar and comfortable with not knowing can also allow a more complete and satisfying experience of life as it is. Since we usually don't know much more than we do know, the space of not knowing is where much of life is actually happening.

Right now, do you really know how your heart manages to beat so regularly? Do you really know how electricity works, where your life is going, how to grow as a person, what love really is, who to trust, and why you are here? And yet, your heart is beating, electricity does seem to work, your life is going somewhere, you somehow seem to grow, love and trust do happen, and you are here. All of these experiences are not contained in or dependent on your knowledge, and yet they are happening and add tremendously to the richness of your life.

Still, we struggle against not knowing. We push ourselves to learn more and more. We strain and strive to know as much as we can. All this struggling and striving is a source of suffering. But what if not knowing, by itself, is a perfectly fine sensation? Only when we struggle against the experience of not knowing and want to know when we can't does the experience of not knowing become painful.

Letting ourselves not know can be a profound relief from the struggle. It also opens up our awareness more fully because we tend to pay attention when we don't know. In the blank space of not knowing is a natural curiosity and hunger for the truth. This curious hunger is an alive and ever-changing experience of the richness of all that can be known and all that is beyond our usual ways of knowing.

PART 3

Exploration Through Inquiry

SELF-INQUIRY

Q: From what I understand, 'enlightenment' is more the dissolution of something false that obscures the true reality that is already present than the attainment of a spiritual transformation. If that's true, should one focus more on dissolving their own mental constructs of ego and mind, and if so, what would you recommend as the best method?

A: You are correct in your description of enlightenment as the uncovering of what is already here rather than the attainment of something. However, I would suggest that there are two ways to approach this process. The first approach is dissolving the structures of the ego, as you mentioned. For this, there are several wonderful forms of directed inquiry, such as *The Sedona Method* or *The Work*, developed by Byron Katie.

The second approach is the exploration of your underlying nature through the technique of self-inquiry, or asking the question, "Who am I?" Self-inquiry is not an intellectual exercise, where you try to figure out the answer with your mind. Instead, this question is meant to direct your awareness back to the sense of *I* so that you come to rest your awareness on this deeply mysterious sense of *I am* or *I exist*. You rest with awareness on your Self and meet whatever unfolds. There are many dimensions to your true nature, including the absolute emptiness of Being, so this exploration is truly endless.

These two approaches, inquiring into your ego and inquiring into the sense of I, are complementary. One isn't better or more important than the other. And these two approaches can be combined in an open-ended exploration of whatever is present right now. If your ego is being triggered and your sense of self is contracted, then it makes sense to explore some of the reactions and beliefs of that ego to at least loosen them a bit. And when you're not experiencing those reactions, it makes sense to rest and experience the I. Inquire into whatever is most present in your experience right now, whether it's the ego or the sense of I. That's what most needs to be seen and accepted. If you meet what's here right now by experiencing it, inquiring into it, and loving it, then the deeper intelligence of your Being will take care of all the rest.

There is no best way to inquire because any way is great! The only art or subtlety to inquiry is in applying it to whatever is here right now, including any fears, resistance, and conditioning, and all the depth and richness of the many dimensions of your true nature. By the way, the point of inquiry isn't enlightenment. The point is the incredible richness of the inquiry itself. The journey is the destination. If you do get to an enlightened place, the unfolding continues even then in ever new and surprising ways.

BEING PRESENT TO FEELINGS

Q: *There's a compulsion that seems to stem from a sense of lack that compels me to feel a need to become better than I am, to grow, to evolve, to reach my highest potential. Sometimes it is veiled in spirituality, but I think it is a sense of lack, a sense of insufficiency and fear that this insufficiency will cause me to be abandoned, treated badly, or suffer. Something tells me I have to be special to survive or get my needs met; something tells me I have to be better than I am and better than others. This prevents me from simply relaxing and being what I am, which is effortless. What we are is effortless being. I know this, but I'm still working my ass off to become something better!*

I feel a sense of hopelessness, but maybe this hopelessness is also a letting go. I realize that letting go is what is ultimately needed, but I don't know how to surrender. I guess what I am is surrender itself when I am relaxed enough to see it. What are your impressions? How do I navigate these waters?

A: It's okay to be working your ass off trying to become better. There's no harm done, and it's often when we've failed utterly at trying to be better that something else moves within us. Surrender isn't something you do. It's really something that happens to you.

In the meantime, you can be very curious about the whole experience of struggle and fear. The more present you are to it just the way it is, the more awareness itself can transform the experience. Your only job is to be as present to it all as much as possible and to be with the feelings as much as you can. This strengthens your capacity to be with your feelings as they arise without suppressing or expressing them. Then when Presence and surrender reveal themselves, you'll be able to stay with that experience as well. The more you practice being present to your feelings and whatever else you are experiencing, the easier it gets.

Suffering is only a problem when we think it's a problem. Once you no longer see suffering as a problem, then it's no longer suffering. Suffering is like a mirage: When you get closer to it, you see that it doesn't exist. All your struggle can't help but eventually bring you closer to the suffering itself, where you'll start to see its nature. Then you'll find yourself more and more able to rest within the difficult patterns and see that they are just ideas, mirages in your own mind.

HOW LONG TO INQUIRE INTO FEELINGS

Q: I feel like I'm getting the hang of being with fear, anger, and other difficult emotions. It's a kind of burning, and I've been noticing the thought or story associated with the feeling, then letting go of the thoughts and letting it burn. When I do this, I find that the difficult emotion is really just energy, and when I allow it, it's actually invigorating.

My question is how do I know how long to stay with the feeling? Sometimes it turns to pure energy and goes away. Other times, with more deeply rooted emotions, it doesn't go away. When it doesn't go away, should I try to devote hours to being with it? Sometimes I'll sit with a feeling for a while, but then I'll have to go to work or attend to other everyday matters. I can still allow the feeling, but it's more difficult to concentrate and fully allow it when other things are going on.

A: Every experience is unique. When you stay with, or inquire into, a feeling, sometimes the energy of it releases or dissolves and a deeper level or dimension of your inner experience is revealed. Or you might find an essential quality, such as peace or joy. Other times, you find another feeling under the one that is releasing. Or maybe not much happens at all. In every case, the inquiry is working perfectly. There's a deep intelligence within your Being that knows exactly how to unfold each inquiry. The more you can just stay with whatever is happening in the inquiry and let go of any ideas or expectations about what is supposed to happen, the more this inner intelligence can work.

When you're doing inquiry, I invite you to follow whatever feels true in terms of how long to stay with this process and how to balance it with the other demands of your life. Remember: The truth is whatever opens your heart and expands your being and whatever quiets your mind. So just notice if it feels true to stay with a feeling a little longer or if it feels truer to move on to another activity. And of course, you can always continue to keep some of your awareness on your inner experiences even as you engage in other activities.

The real value of staying with and inquiring into feelings isn't the results you experience. The point of being with feelings isn't to resolve or get rid of them, even though this kind of open-ended inquiry can have that effect. The real point of this practice is to realize the powerful mystery of awareness itself. What is this that can notice and observe a feeling? What does it mean that you can choose to stay with a feeling? What is awareness? What is aware?

Spiritual seekers are often so busy digging for some imagined buried treasure that they don't notice that the shovel they're digging with (awareness) is covered with large diamonds and rubies. The treasure is already in your hands! What a miracle this attention is that you use to stay with a feeling. Don't overlook the immense value of the awareness that is already here in every moment.

INQUIRY INTO NUMBNESS

Q: *I have had many disappointments this past year, and I lost my job, but I don't feel anything. I have been numb for some time, and I can't figure out whether it's because I've reached a level of consciousness where I'm in control of my thoughts or whether it's a defense mechanism. I get sad thoughts sometimes for not having a job, but these thoughts are washed away by other thoughts: "You didn't cause this. You're doing what you can to change things. What's the point anyway? I'm so tired of fighting," followed by numbness.*

A: Only you can tell if the numbness is a defense mechanism. The truth about this and anything else is whatever opens your Heart and quiets your mind. Does your Heart feel open when you are numb? Does your mind quiet down? If so, then you can just rest in your Heart.

If the opposite is happening (your awareness contracts and your mind gets busy), that is a sign that something is being avoided. That isn't bad. Thank God for all of our defense mechanisms. None of us would have survived this far without them!

If this numbness is an avoidance, then it is an opportunity to be curious about it. What is it like when you are numb? What are the actual sensations of "numbness"? Are the sensations bad, or are they just sensations? What happens if you shine your awareness on the numb feeling without trying to get rid of or change it in any way? Inquiring in this way can gradually uncover what is happening more fully. Again, there's nothing wrong with a defense mechanism, but since it's happening, you might as well find out as much as you can about it.

I also invite you to become very curious about when the numbness arises. Does it come with the thought, "You didn't cause this. You are doing what you can to change things"? Or does it come more with the thought, "What's the point anyway?" Also notice what's happening in your Heart when you aren't thinking about your life at all and just experiencing the moment as it is.

The truth is what opens, relaxes, or softens your sense of being, your Heart. Each and every moment is a new opportunity to discover more about the truth. A contracted, numb feeling is telling you something about your experience. When your Heart contracts, it is working perfectly to tell you that your current thought, feeling, or desire isn't very true or important.

INQUIRY INTO A BROKEN HEART

Q: *I now know that my friend doesn't love me. I feel like a part of me has died. Nothing I've tried has eased the enormous pain in my chest. What can I do?*

A: Loss is like that. It just hurts. Even when there's nothing you can do to relieve the pain, you still might want to explore the experience you're having. Specifically, I invite you to explore the part of you that feels like it has died. What is that like? If, for just a moment, you completely allow that part of you to feel dead, is that actually a bad sensation, or just a dead sensation? Suffering always comes from rejection of our experience and sensations, not from the experience and sensations themselves, even the most intense and enormous feelings.

It can help to allow the pain to be bigger than your body. There's no need to contain it within your chest. Just let it be as big as it needs to be.

And then be curious. What's the pain like? Exactly where do you feel it? How big is it? What else is present besides the pain? If there's a feeling of deadness or emptiness, what is that like? What is present in the empty space? What is present inside the deadness?

The point of these questions isn't to get rid of the pain, but to help you discover that it's okay to feel pain. The deepest healing is always to find out that there's nothing here that needs to be healed. Pain is natural and normal after a loss, and yet you don't need to suffer from the pain. Just let the pain be here, and you may discover that you are okay even if your heart is broken. Your heart can be broken wide open without actually damaging anything because your true Heart cannot be broken. It is big enough to hold all of the pain and loss.

INQUIRY INTO CONTROL

Q: *I think that wanting to control everything in one's life is bad. Wanting to make things happen a certain way is a cause for suffering, and it is an attachment. I want to control things in my life. I want to control myself and break my bad habits. I want to make certain things happen a certain way. But I don't want to have to go through the suffering that comes with that need to control. I was hoping that you could help me reconcile one's ability to make things happen and to be the cause and effect of one's life without being afraid of the potential loss and suffering that may come from that.*

A: It would be easier if there were a simple answer to the whole question of control. If trying to control was really just a bad thing, then we all would have given it up a long time ago! But trying to control is a natural impulse because it works sometimes. For a behavior to be reinforced, it only has to work some of the time. So it's natural that we try to control things, even though doing so only works occasionally and therefore often leads to wasted effort and even suffering.

The truth is we are both in control and out of control in life. That is the nature of duality on this level of reality. However, that still isn't the whole truth about control.

If we are not completely in control, then what is? Is life really just a bunch of random events, including the random interactions of a bunch of apparent beings with free will, all trying to control things but only succeeding sometimes? Or is there also a greater, wiser Presence that affects what happens? What if a Divine Intelligence is unfolding life? Are we in control or out of control then?

Behind all of the events of life is a deeper wisdom. It knows what needs to happen, and it manages most of the time to succeed in bringing that about. I say "most of the time" because this greater intelligence isn't really in a hurry to get anywhere and it has all of eternity to do what it does. It likes the surprises and twists and turns that apparent egos bring to the drama of life, so it lets them interfere to a degree. This is because it knows that no harm can really be done and also because it eventually finds a way to get where it's going anyway.

A friend of mine has one of those navigation systems in his car that tells you where to turn. I asked him what happens if you don't turn when it tells you to. He said that for a while it would try to get you to turn around and turn where you should have. However, he said, if you don't do that, it will calculate a new route to where you were headed and start giving you directions based on your having not turned. This deeper intelligence is like that. It lets you succeed or fail at trying to control things, and then it picks up from there and makes what really needs to happen, happen.

So there is a dynamic interplay between the capacity of our ego to control things and the capacity of Being to control things. What a formula for surprises, mystery, and drama that is! And then there are all of the other apparent people trying to control things also! What a crazy dance!

When we are able to hold this larger perspective in regard to our efforts to control, a natural loosening of our grip on the steering wheel of life happens. Why try so hard to control everything when there are so many forces at play? This perspective may not cause you to give up trying to control things entirely, but it will ease your suffering around this issue. Those efforts are natural, but they aren't that important. You steer to the best of your ability, but then you let go of the results. Sometimes you get where you wanted to go, and sometimes you don't. Sometimes you even end up somewhere better than where you wanted to go!

Maybe the ego and all its efforts at control are just a necessary developmental stage. Once you, as an ego, have gone as far as you can with your own efforts, you reach a point where you can only go further by surrendering. And yet, surrendering isn't something you, as an ego, can do. The ego can only experience the dilemma of its impulse to effort and its seeing of the futility of effort until something else moves that we call surrender.

What is here beyond your own effort? What is here right now that doesn't need to be controlled? In just holding the questions without trying for an answer, another dimension of experience can sometimes be revealed that is full of peace, joy, and love. This is not a place of no control or a place of control, but something that opens up beyond the whole experience of control.

It is here that the suffering from our efforts to control is truly resolved into an enjoyment of the whole dance of our life. Loss is just one more twist and turn in the dance. Effort is just done for the sake of moving and dancing. There is nowhere to go and nowhere to not go, nothing to do and nothing to not do.

EXPLORING EMPTINESS

Sometimes we feel an inner sense of emptiness. When we look within, it seems like nothing is there, so we distract ourselves with something on the outside, like food or television. And yet, these outer distractions take care of the emptiness only temporarily; they capture our attention only temporarily. When the distraction is over, the emptiness returns.

What is it about emptiness that makes us want to move away from it? Is emptiness really a bad sensation? When you consider the literal meaning of emptiness, how can it be a problem? Is it possible for "nothing" to hurt you? Is that sense of emptiness, that empty feeling, actually uncomfortable, or is the restlessness and activity of trying to distract yourself or avoid the emptiness what is uncomfortable?

This is an important distinction. We are so used to assuming that feelings of lack, emptiness, or something missing are a problem that we are uncomfortable when that is our experience. But is the emptiness the source of our discomfort? Or is what we do in response to the emptiness the source of our discomfort, including the stories we tell ourselves and the judgments about the fact that we feel empty?

It's not our fault that we tend to avoid feelings of emptiness. We were taught to do this by everyone around us who was doing it. In fact, there's a good reason to avoid one feeling of emptiness—the feeling of hunger—since we need to eat when we're hungry. However, we often interpret a feeling of lack as a need for food. Have you ever eaten when you weren't hungry to try to distract or relieve yourself from a feeling? It's possible to simply experience the sensations of emptiness or lack and discover that they aren't so bad. Try it and see for yourself:

Exercise: What happens right now if you just allow any sensation you might have of emptiness, lack, or there not being enough? Are those sensations painful, or are they just sensations? Perhaps there's something in particular that feels lacking: a lack of strength, energy, or self-worth; a lack of excitement or interest; a sense of there not being enough security or safety; or a feeling that right now there's no joy or happiness. And yet, are the sensations that let you know that these things seem to be missing unpleasant? What happens if you just let those sensations be here for a moment?

It certainly would simplify life if we didn't have to do anything about these feelings of lack. So much of our activity, effort, and inner striving are meant to get us more of what we seem to lack. But what if it's okay to lack something? What if it's okay to just feel empty? What a relief! So much less to do!

Even more surprising is discovering that the sensations of emptiness can be enjoyed. There is a richness to silence, to stillness, to space itself. We overlook the richness of the inner silent spaces in our being. Most of us are quite unfamiliar with them because we've been turning away from them most of our lives. Just as a wine connoisseur can make finer distinctions in the flavor and quality of wine than someone who has only tasted wine a few times, we can become connoisseurs of emptiness.

Perhaps the biggest surprise is when we discover that the very thing that feels lacking in an experience of emptiness is often found in the emptiness itself. For example, if you feel weak or lacking in strength and energy and you stay present to that sensation of weakness or lack, you may notice a deeper, more subtle sense of strength appearing in the emptiness.

The strength, joy, peace, and love that can be found in the empty places within us are much more subtle than the feelings generated from our usual attempts to feel strong, happy, or loving. However, when we focus on the inner strength, joy, peace, or love, the experience of them can become powerful and real in a way that far exceeds our expectations. Who knew that there was a deep reservoir of infinite peace lying under the restless feeling of a lack of peace? What a surprise to find abundant joy in the dry, empty sense of a lack of excitement and fun?

This principle—that strength, joy, peace, and love can be found inside our feelings of emptiness and lack—is a radical new perspective. But this truth can only be fully known by diving into your experiences of emptiness. Since doing this is so contrary to our conditioning, we have to develop a new habit of paying attention to feelings of emptiness in order to discover the richness waiting there.

This would be easier to do if every time you turned your awareness toward a feeling of emptiness or lack, you were immediately filled with a sense of abundant peace or joy. But the experience of emptiness is many-layered, like an onion. So as you move into a particular feeling of emptiness, you may find a deep sense of strength or love, or you may uncover a deeper layer of conditioning. Initially, the sense of emptiness or lack might get worse. As you allow the feeling of there not being enough or of being inadequate to just be there, painful memories or a strong aversion to the sensation of emptiness may be triggered, which can make it difficult to keep your attention on the emptiness itself. Whenever you're distracted or find yourself avoiding the sense of something lacking, you might miss an opportunity to discover a little more about the nature of that emptiness, including any subtle quality to be found there. A new habit of staying with each new layer of feeling and memory and possibly even stronger sensations of emptiness and incompleteness needs to be developed. There's nothing you can do to make the feelings of peace and joy appear except to stay with your experience, no matter what is showing up, until they do.

Exercise: *Notice what you're feeling inside right now. Especially note any sense of emptiness or lack, such as a lack of worthiness, capability, clarity, understanding, or a lack of peace, joy, or love. For now, just allow any sense of lack to be here. Notice how you experience the sense of lack. Where is it located? How big is the empty space? What are the sensations associated with it? Is the emptiness itself uncomfortable, or is it just empty? Keep paying attention to the empty feeling and notice what happens next. Are thoughts or memories arising? Is it easy or hard to stay with the experience you are having? Remember to drop into your Heart or give space to the feelings, as this can help you stay with your experience. Know that whatever arises next is exactly what you need to experience for now. If a painful memory or uncomfortable emotion is triggered, just stay with that as best you can. Notice if there's an even deeper sense of emptiness or lack in each emotion that arises.*

If a strong desire or urge to move away or distract yourself arises, just stay with that urge. Again, notice if there's a deeper or bigger sense of emptiness behind or beneath the desire to distract or move away. Especially be curious about the empty spaces or direct sensations of lack that you discover as you stay with your experience. Are the empty spaces painful or just empty? What qualities does the space itself have? Is it moving or still? Does it have a color? Is it clear or foggy? How big or deep is the emptiness?

When your attention is simply on the empty space itself, you may notice something present or moving within the space. What is present in the center of the space where something is lacking? Is there any peace in the emptiness? Is there any joy or happiness? Is there any love? Set aside any expectations of what that peace, joy, or love should look like and just be curious about any that you find. Especially set aside any expectations about how big or strong the feeling should be and just be curious about even the smallest sense of strength, clarity, or peace that is present. Notice what happens as you pay attention to the center of the emptiness. Does the feeling of peace or joy get stronger, or does touching into peace or joy trigger an even deeper longing and sense of lack? Stay with whatever arises for as long as you can. If any strong emotions or desires are stirred up by this exercise, take some time to just rest and settle after you stop exploring. This can be intense and difficult work, and it's important to nurture yourself in the process.

The most surprising and liberating discovery is to find that everything that really matters in life, such as peace, joy, strength, power, clarity, value or worth, support, nourishment, and love, can be found within you—and not just when you're lucky enough to be already experiencing them, but also when it seems like they're absent and have never been there. Once you've discovered them in the sense of lack and incompleteness many times, it becomes possible to relax and know they're always there, no matter what the present moment feels like.

This is the key discovery: Experiences of our true nature come and go like every other experience, but to know that love is here in all its glory even when you're experiencing the absence of it frees us from struggle and suffering. To know that everything you could ever want or need is already here, even when you're experiencing the opposite, frees you from having to have a particular inner or outer experience to be happy. Knowing the true potential of inner space or emptiness means you can trust that everything is fine even if you aren't experiencing any peace, joy, or love. The potential to experience peace, joy, and love is always there.

The love and joy that are experienced can never capture the infinite potential of the source of love and joy within us. Because this peace, love, and joy can never be exhausted, you can just relax and know that they are here, where they can never be lost or used up. Enjoy them while they appear, and enjoy the stillness and spaciousness that remain when there isn't a particular manifestation of Presence, or Being, appearing.

SEEKING HAPPINESS

Q: *Do we seek happiness because of a void, or is it our nature to long for more?*

A: We do seek, first, for happiness and something better and then for spiritual truth to try to fill the void, or emptiness, within. But both are doomed to failure because everything we put in the emptiness and every experience we have are dissolved back into emptiness. Trying to fill the emptiness is like trying to fill a bucket with lots of holes—it never fills up no matter how much water we put in!

Eventually after massive amounts of failure, we get so tired of seeking and trying to find happiness that we finally just let ourselves experience the emptiness itself. What is emptiness like? Is emptiness a bad sensation? What is present in the emptiness? What are the qualities of the emptiness itself? One of the many surprises you discover is that joy and happiness actually flow out of the emptiness. When seeking stops, it's possible to notice the happiness and peace that are present in the emptiness and actually present in every moment.

If you're still seeking or wanting something, including happiness, then usually the best thing to do is keep seeking. The worst that can happen is you'll wear yourself out even sooner! But it's also possible that you're already exhausted enough from seeking to just rest and let yourself be empty. Some joy, peace, or love may be noticed in that emptiness, or the experience of emptiness may trigger another round of trying to fill the emptiness, which will just wear you out some more.

When happiness appears, just pay attention to it: Where is it really coming from? Does getting or knowing something really make you happy, or does it just allow you to rest for a moment and finally experience the happiness that has always been there? Does happiness ever show up even when you don't get what you want? Is happiness there when you're just still for a moment and you finally let yourself be empty? Eventually, you discover that you can trust the emptiness more than your seeking.

FINDING CONNECTION IN LONELINESS

Q: *I'm learning to look deeply at my loneliness now and sit with it. That's very helpful. Yet, the loneliness comes up when I want to connect with others. Maybe because of a certain energy, because of karmas, because someone is judging me, or for some other reason, I feel there's a lack of connection with others.*

A: Maybe I can add a bit of insight into the last thing you mentioned, which is the lack of a sense of connection. We are so deeply conditioned to look for connection (and everything else) on the outside. We want others to act or speak a certain way so that we will feel connected with them, when in fact, the place where we are connected with others is deep within ourselves. Being connected to our own Being is where the connection lies, and that connection is available even when someone is judging or rejecting us.

When someone likes us and responds positively to us, we are able to relax and just be ourselves around them. This naturalness allows us to connect with our own Being. The sense of connection you long for comes from being connected to your true nature. That is always where the sense of connection comes from, even when it seems like we need others to love and approve of us to feel that connection. It's just easier to feel connected when others respond positively to us because it allow us to relax and feel our own connection with Source.

This feeling of a lack of connection is a fruitful area for inquiry. Who knows what you might find if you become curious about this sense of a lack of connection. Where is the lack felt in your body? What is present in the empty space where connection seems lacking? While you never know what you'll discover when you inquire into a sense of lack, often you find the very thing you thought you were lacking! What a surprise to discover that the empty space inside you is itself connected to everyone and everything!

INQUIRY INTO RESENTMENT

Q: *How do I move beyond resentment to forgiveness?*

A: It's not a question of one or the other, of having resentment *or* forgiveness. There's room in your awareness for both resentment *and* forgiveness. Just let all your resentment be here just the way it is. And then also look to see if there's anything else here besides resentment and hurt. Is there also space here? As big as your feelings of resentment may seem, how big are they compared to space itself? Obviously there's a lot more space here than resentment or any other feeling. When I say space, I'm talking about all of the space, time (which is another dimension of space), and awareness in the universe and beyond. That's probably quite a bit bigger than even your biggest resentments!

What a relief! You don't have to get rid of, solve, or fix your resentment to also experience forgiveness. Resentment is natural and normal. You can feel it just as much as you feel it. Then notice all of the space around your resentment, and also notice what else is here in that space. That's where you'll find forgiveness and everything else you might seek. Space is the softest, most allowing, most tender thing there is. Right now, it is holding you and all your resentments and doubts in a totally accepting embrace. Notice that space is allowing your resentment. Space does nothing to stop you from feeling or even expressing resentment. What a strange and ever-present quality space is! It isn't choosy. It doesn't love this and not love that. It loves and allows everything!

Once you notice that space allows your resentment totally, then you might be able to notice that there's also space for the people or actions you're resenting. Space allows them to do the things you resent, and it allows you to resent them.

You may wonder, so what? Everything is allowed by space. So what? Well, if you want to experience your true nature, you may want to get curious about this strange thing called space. If you want to experience the infinite capacity for forgiveness that your consciousness naturally has, then you may want to become curious about the loving softness of empty space. That is where forgiveness comes from. That is what is able to forgive and able to love, in part because space has nothing to lose. It loves and allows everything because it can't be harmed. And it turns out that everything that really matters in life comes from emptiness or space: love, forgiveness, joy, compassion, strength, clarity, inspiration, pleasure, satisfaction, and more.

We can discover the nature of space by exploring this mystery that there is space for everything. Why is there so much room in this universe and within our consciousness? Where did all this infinite space come from? You don't need to search for space. It's right here. You are in it. It permeates you, or you permeate it, depending on how you look at it. And anywhere you look, there's more space. Physical objects are actually made up mostly of space. Even subatomic particles appear more like space than like things.

Is it possible that things are really space? What if everything is just one space that vibrates at different frequencies or has condensed into different densities, depending on whether we're seeing emptiness, energy, or matter? What if all there is, is space? All of your questions about forgiveness, resentment, and anything else point back to this one thing called space. That is where all the answers lie.

And, of course, if all there is, is space, then that is what you are also.

DOING INQUIRY WHEN YOU GET TRIGGERED

Q: *When there's a strong aversion to a person, sometimes feelings dissolve into that space, and at other times, this doesn't happen and leads to outbursts. Is it better to physically withdraw or should one continue taking up the challenge to look from within every time that feeling of aversion comes up even if it leads to expression of the feeling? Is there such a thing as a congenial environment for self-inquiry?*

A: As with most things in life, there's no formula for how to act when someone or something is triggering your emotions. Every situation is unique, and so it can be helpful to develop a capacity for a wide range of responses. Sometimes you'll be able to inquire while you are in the situation that triggered you, and sometimes you'll need to leave that situation before you can inquire effectively. On occasion, expressing a feeling opens up the interaction to a deeper level, while other times, doing that just causes hurt or confusion. If you're having an emotional reaction that could lead to an outburst, leaving the situation and continuing the inquiry while you're alone might be best. It makes sense to leave the situation if staying is causing you or others to contract even more. If you stay and get more contracted, then your inquiry may not go very deep.

There is no wrong time for inquiry. If you can inquire when you are getting triggered, that's great. If you can't inquire then but later, when you're alone, that's great. When you first begin practicing inquiry, it's often easier to do it when you're alone and it's quiet. Then as you become more familiar with inquiry, it will be easier to inquire in a wider range of situations.

What's true in any moment has a solidity and depth to it that is undeniable when it is experienced. As I often say, the truth is whatever opens your Heart and quiets your mind. Something that is less true has the opposite effect: It contracts your Heart, makes your mind busy, and has a feeling of unreality or superficiality. So in the day-to-day living of your life, try to sense these reactions to gain some perspective about how true your reactions are and also how true it felt or would feel to act a certain way in response to being triggered.

TWO PATHS TO LOVE

Q: *There is such a great need in me to be appreciated by other people, by my friends for example, and I'm never satisfied. I never get enough appreciation, and because of that I suffer a lot. What can I do?*

A: Even when we clearly see our conditioning at work and how much suffering it causes, it can still be difficult to shift out of a particular way of feeling and acting. I have two suggestions to offer you.

The first is to experiment with giving love to everything and everyone. It is actually by giving love or approval that we are filled with a sense of loving Presence, not by getting love or approval from others. True love is open acceptance or space and a fullness of attention or noticing. What we really want from a lover is someone who lets us be the way we are but who also wants to see and know everything about us. So I would suggest you give this same acceptance and noticing to everything you experience. It's easiest to start with neutral or pleasant things, so try practicing on simple objects. Notice a piece of furniture and then give it a lot of space to just be the way it is. Or you can notice that there is already a lot of space for it. As you notice the space around the furniture, also notice everything you can about the furniture. What are its qualities? How does it reflect light? How does it feel? What are the specific details of its construction and appearance? Shower it with attention and see if you can notice even subtle aspects of it that you never noticed before.

Then move on to another object and then on to another experience after that, perhaps the sound of the wind or a sensation in your body. Start with simple, neutral things and then gradually add in things that are more challenging to love, such as a sensation you don't like or an object that has negative associations. Finally, you can experiment with giving this free flowing space and attention to other people.

As you do this, notice how you feel. How does it feel to give the most precious thing you have—awareness—to other objects, sensations, and people? Do you ever run out, or can you give and give awareness and still have more to give? Even if you encounter something you can't love in this way, you can simply give love to the sensation inside you of being blocked or resistant to loving. The trick is to give love to *whatever* you are experiencing, even if it's a judgment or feeling of resistance. Accept and notice your judgment of the other person, and then you may find that you can also accept and notice the person.

In this way, you discover that all the love you want from others is already inside you. We are filled with love when we give love to others, not when we receive it from others. But to really trust this, you may need many experiences of this limitless flow of love.

The other suggestion I have for you is to let yourself really feel the lack of love inside you. Even when you know you can give and give love, there will still be times when you don't experience the flow of love. In those moments, what you experience is an emptiness. The place that all this love comes from inside you is completely empty, so we tend to not want to feel it, since it doesn't seem very promising to feel something so dry and empty. And yet, what is that empty space you've been trying to fill up with attention from others actually like? Is it dark or bright? Is it heavy or light? Is it clear or foggy or obscured somehow? How deep is the emptiness? Can you find a bottom to it?

This emptiness at your core is the source of everything that really matters in life: love, peace, joy, wisdom, clarity, strength, satisfaction, and existence itself. What a surprising place to find everything you have ever wanted—in the emptiness at your core. And yet, that is the only place from which you will ever be satisfied. It is by discovering everything about this emptiness—every quality it has, every nuance of its expression—that we can finally be content. You will never be done discovering its endless nature, but at some point, you will be able to trust that everything that really matters is already inside of you.

By returning again and again to the emptiness, you keep your attention on the true source of what you seek. Sometimes you find an even deeper sense of emptiness when you look within, but then is emptiness really a bad sensation? Or is it just empty? Does emptiness ever really hurt? How can "nothing" ever hurt? Other times, you'll discover one of the precious qualities of your Being arising, such as love, peace, or joy. What a surprising place to find them! By returning again and again to your own empty nature, you finally learn to trust that you have everything you need and that you don't need anything from others.

Seeking love from the outside is an old habit that you were taught to do by everyone around you who was doing the same thing. The best way to counteract an old habit that no longer serves you is to develop a new habit or even several new habits that work even better than the old one. In this case, the new habits are to give love to everything and to look within the emptiness at your core. Once you've done this often enough for it to become a habit, then check to see if you have enough love and enough peace, acceptance, and joy. The true source of these things is within you.

LOVING HOW HARD IT IS TO LOVE

Q: So what would you say is the most effective and simple way to open one's Heart?

A: The simplest thing is to give love. Just give love to objects, sensations, your own body, the trees, the clouds, thoughts, feelings—whatever your awareness lands on.

Q: The idea of giving everything love is appealing, and I understand it theoretically, but to be able to do it is another story.

A: It helps if you strip love down to its essence, which is awareness and space, or noticing and allowing. You don't have to like something to give it space to be here and to notice what it's like. And at the same time you can give space and awareness to your not liking it. You can love not liking something!

Q: That sounds so hard. I've tried things like that before, but I lose my boundaries and start accepting things I shouldn't, which only leads to conflict with myself and others.

A: There are two keys to loving everything in awareness. One is to love whatever is present right now. So when it's hard to love, then simply love how hard loving is. You just allow and be curious about the experience of how hard loving is. How do you know it's hard? What is that like in your body? If you were going to teach me how to make it hard for me to love something that is hard for you to love, what would you have to teach me to do?

The other key is to include everything that arises in your experience, especially everything that arises within yourself. The problem with boundaries often occurs when we don't include our own feelings and preferences. When you love these as much as you love the things arising in the world and in other people, then you can naturally act in a way that takes care of yourself as well as others. It's not that you can completely avoid conflict this way, but you are very present to any conflict or difficulty that appears, so you respond to it appropriately and, at the same time, open your heart and love it. Since life already has plenty of conflict, why not experience it with open, loving awareness?

PART 4

Oneness

ONENESS

Advaita is a Sanskrit word meaning "not two" and points to the fundamental oneness of everything—that everything is a part of and made of one substance. Often the question arises, "If it is all one thing, why don't I experience it that way?" This is confusing oneness for the appearance of sameness. Things can appear different without being separate. Just look at your hand for a moment. Your fingers are all different from each other, but are they separate? They all arise from the same hand. Similarly, the objects, animals, plants and people in the world are all definitely different in their appearance and functioning. But they are all connected at their source—they come from the same source. This one Being that is behind all life has an infinite number of different expressions that we experience as different objects.

To continue with the hand analogy, your fingers are all made of the same substance. They are made up of similar tissues, cells, atoms, and at the deepest level, subatomic particles. Similarly, when your experience of reality becomes more subtle, you discover that everything is just different expressions of one field of Being.

What about your experience right now? Is it possible to discover this subtle oneness in ordinary experience? It is, if you set aside the expectation of a dramatic experience of oneness and explore the oneness a little bit at a time. Just as even a single drop of water is wet, you can experience oneness in even simple everyday experiences, since oneness is a fundamental quality of everything that exists.

As an experiment, just notice your fingers and the palm of your hand. Can you say where one starts and the other ends, or are they one thing? To take this further, where does your hand stop and your forearm begin? Can you experience the oneness of your hand and your forearm? If these are not separate, then what about other parts of your body? Are your feet and your ears really one even though they are so different? Now notice if there really is a separation between your thoughts and your head. Where does your head stop and something else called thought begin? What about feelings or desires? Are they really separate from you or your body?

Now, notice the simple sensations you are having: the sounds you are hearing, the sensations of touch, and the objects and events you are seeing. If you are seeing something, where does the seeing stop and something else called the eye begin? If you are hearing sounds, where does the sound start and the ear stop? Perhaps the hearing, the sound, and your ear are all one thing. Yes, the ear is different from the sound, but in the act of hearing, they become one thing.

Then, where does the source of the sound stop and the sound itself start? For example, if a bird is singing outside your window, where does the bird stop and the sound of its song begin? Or are they one thing? If the bird and its song are one thing, and your hearing and the song are one thing, then is it possible that you and the bird are also one thing?

Oneness has often been thought of as something hidden or difficult to experience, when it is quite ordinary and available in every moment. Of course, a dramatic experience of oneness is a rare event. But why wait for something so rare when this sweet and satisfying oneness is right here, right now?

MULTIPLE EXPERIENCERS WITHIN ONENESS

Q: *How can there only be one experiencer if there are multiple experiences? Surely there must be multiple experiencers for there to be multiple simultaneous experiences happening in tandem, otherwise who is experiencing the other person's experience? I know I'm not. I'm only experiencing this human experience centered around one human being's sense perceptions and cognitive faculties. I have never witnessed another person's experience, so how can we be One and the same?*

A: How can one thing also be many things? This is one of the deepest mysteries. It would appear that these apparent individual selves are here for a purpose, maybe just to have individual experiences. Imagine what it would be like if you, as Oneness, were experiencing everything that exists and has ever existed. That would tend to get in the way of having and focusing on a particular experience, so you might choose to limit yourself to a particular experience and perspective. To do this, you might become an individual with a limited awareness. If you, as Oneness, became an individual, you would still have the potential to experience yourself as everything, since ultimately that is what you are. From one perspective you could experience all of reality, and from another perspective you could experience an individual reality.

Since this infinite, aware Being that you are is also eternal, it has a lot of time to fill. So it loves to try on different perspectives and experiences and is even willing to try on perspectives that last a lifetime or many lifetimes. It has nothing to lose, since it can't lose the capacity or potential to expand into a more limitless perspective when it chooses to.

The truth isn't limited to our ability to understand and conceptualize it, so two seemingly opposite things can both be true.

Perhaps an individual expression of infinite Being experiences a limited range of awareness, and at the same time, a greater dimension of the same Being is experiencing all of it. Both are true, and both perspectives are always here and available in every moment along with an infinite variety of perspectives in between these two extremes. There isn't a right perspective or a wrong perspective for awareness to take. It seems to want to try them all.

HOW TO EXPERIENCE ONENESS MORE DEEPLY

Q: *I know intellectually that I am Awareness. I say "intellectually" because I don't yet sense it as fact. Do you have any additional pointers?*

A: Many people have grasped the Oneness and their true nature as Awareness intellectually, but it is not a common or an ongoing experience for them. It seems there is often a gap between an intellectual knowing and a more grounded, knowing-in-your-being kind of knowing. The bridge between these two is, very simply, repeated experiences of Awareness. We tend to only really know something we have experienced a lot.

For everyone, different amounts of experience are required for that knowing to be felt in an ongoing way. How many times would it take to do something like flying an airplane before you felt you knew how to do it? If you piloted an airplane once for two minutes, would you feel you knew how to fly an airplane? Hopefully not! But if you had flown solo hundreds of times, you would probably have an ongoing sense that you know how to fly an airplane.

So having a deeper experience of Oneness is usually a matter of having lots of experiences of Oneness and Presence. However, it can also result from one very strong or long lasting experience. Although everyone would like to have a single big experience that does the trick, from my many conversations with people, more often this shift seems to happen gradually, as a result of a series of experiences.

There is one more point I'd like to share with you. Experiences of Oneness are wonderful and of great service to this shift, but such experiences are not that important in and of themselves. Like every other experience, the experience of Oneness comes and goes. And any effort to get or keep such an experience will cause you to suffer as much as striving to get or keep any other experience.

While it's profoundly delightful to experience Oneness, a deep knowing of the truth is what matters. When there is a deep knowing that Presence, or Being, is all there is and that is who you are, it no longer matters if you're experiencing it in this moment or not. It is similar to how while it is useful to own an automobile, imagine if you had to experience your car twenty-four hours a day in order to own a car! Owning a car is much easier than that since you trust the existence of your car, even if you can't see it in this moment. We have had enough experiences of the reality of physical objects that we have developed a trust in them, which allows us to freely move in and out of experiences of our car without doubting that it will still be there when we need it.

In the same way, with enough experiences of Oneness, you just trust this deeper reality. Experiences of our true nature are necessary to develop this trust in Oneness, but those experiences don't have to be ongoing for this knowing and trust to become ongoing. The real point of spiritual experiences is for the experience of Oneness to become irrelevant because the deeper sense of knowing is so constant.

There are no techniques or processes that can cause you to experience Oneness or Presence, and there is no formula for the shift to a deeper knowing and trust. However, spiritual practices and teachings can put you in a place of curiosity about and receptivity to the spontaneous arising of Presence. They make it more likely for a spontaneous experience of Oneness or Presence to arise.

ONE SOURCE FOR EVERYTHING

There is just one source for everything. Everything comes from an infinite potential within existence itself. Don't take my word for it—reach out and touch something and, for a moment, just sense its pure existence, the simple fact that it exists. Then sense even more deeply to feel the source of the object. See if you can sense how it is coming into existence freshly in this moment. In every instant, it is a completely new version of itself. You may be able to sense its source directly, not with your mind or through logic, but with your fingertips and your Being.

Now touch another object and see if you can sense its source. Where is its existence flowing from? You can also hold your hand out and feel the space in front of you. First just experience the reality of space with your fingertips. There's a mysterious, open, allowing spaciousness here that everything else fits in. As you sense the wonder of the space in front of you, see if you can also feel its source. Where does space come from? Where is the space itself flowing from? Although you may not be able to sense the source of space by thinking about it or figuring it out, you may be able to directly sense the underlying source of infinite space through your fingertips and your subtle inner sensing. It's a matter of sensing with your whole being the wonder that lies just beyond your fingertips, even when you are only touching empty space.

Now reach down and touch your own body. Once again, just sense the wonder of your body's existence. Then sense the source of that miraculous form you often call "me." Where does the body's existence come from? You can touch your legs, your face, your other hand, your hair, and with each part of your body, see if you can sense from a deeper place the infinite potential that can form itself into a living physical body. It can help to drop down and sense the body from your heart instead of your head. This allows a fuller sensing, with all of your physical and subtle senses.

To whatever degree you have a sense of the source of space and of these various objects, notice if there's any difference or separation between the source of the objects and your body or empty space. Is it the same source that is forming the furniture and your body? Is there any separation between the source of the space around you and the source of your body? Don't worry if this doesn't make logical sense, and simply sense with your heart the source of space and the source of your body at the same time. Are they separate, or are they one and the same?

You can explore further with nonphysical experiences. Notice the flow of thoughts you are having right now. Even though you can't touch your thoughts with your fingers, just sense their existence and their source in infinite potential. Where do thoughts come from? Where does the energy of feelings arise out of? What is the source of your desires? We are often so involved with the content of our thoughts or the object of our desires that we rarely pause to consider their source.

What do you find? It's fine if you only have a vague sense of the source of an object or space or your thoughts. What is this vague sense of the source like? Is it a similar sense for all of the objects and experiences that you explore? Can you find a boundary between the source of your body and the source of your thoughts? Can you find separation between the source of objects and the source of space itself?

Differences and separation are very obvious at the level of form. Your body appears very different and separate from the objects in the room. Your body has very different qualities from the space around you, even if it isn't really separate from the space around you. This is the beauty and wonder of the world of form and experience: It offers endless differences and the appearance of separation. That's what makes it possible for two forms to dance or play. But what about the source of these experiences and forms? At that level are they separate? How pronounced is the difference between the source of your thoughts and the source of your physicality? Do your body and space come from the same subtle Presence that lies behind all experience and differences?

It is at the level of the source of existence that oneness is obvious and clearly true. If we look for oneness in the world of form, we can easily doubt its reality. Often, at best, oneness is a vague concept we try to imagine. But if we sense the source of everything, we find that there is a deeper, infinite potential that everything comes out of and everything is made of. Then, if we continue to sense the underlying source of the various forms, we can more clearly sense their oneness even while we enjoy and appreciate their endless differences.

EVERY MOMENT IS SELF-REALIZATION

Recently, a teacher and friend made a simple comment that the soul is the sum total of all of our experiences. It struck me how this meant that every experience adds to our soul, and there is no experience that can detract from it. Since we share experiences with many other souls, that would mean that our souls overlap. Anywhere our experience overlaps, our souls would also overlap. And since we overlap with so many other souls, ultimately all souls are connected through this sharing of experience.

Every experience is actually an experience of self-realization. In each and every experience, we are realizing a capacity or aspect of our soul, and by extension, an aspect of our true nature as Being. Since all there is, is Being, every experience is an experience of Being. Every experience adds to the totality of our understanding and realization of our true nature. There is no other possibility.

This is a dilemma if we believe there is a better, truer, more spiritual aspect of our Being that we want to be realizing. What if my anger is part of my true nature? What if my greed, lust, fear, sadness, confusion, and pain are all part of my true nature, along with all of the love, peace, and joy that are also part of Being? In hoping and waiting for a better experience, we may be overlooking the significance of our present moment experience, just as it is. It isn't that sadness and greed are equivalent to peace and joy, but every experience has significance, since every experience is an experience of our true nature.

The experiences that we may reject because we think they aren't the correct experience may actually be made up of the same peace, joy, and love we are hoping to have. We think of this world as a world of opposites, or dualities. But if we look more closely, we find that the so-called opposites are really just different amounts of one thing. Light and dark are an example: There is no such thing as dark, only light existing as photons. There are no "darkons." You can't buy a "flashdark" and point it at things and make them disappear. However when there is little or no light, we call that dark, even though there is no such thing. Similarly, the only thing that exists is our true nature, which is filled with joy and love. If we are experiencing little or no joy or love, we may call that sadness or fear, although those are really only the relative absence of joy and love. And of course, there is often some joy in sadness and some love even in fear.

What if every experience is a unique jewel of our multifaceted Being? What if every experience adds to the abundance of our soul and moves us toward the greatness of our true nature? What if what you are experiencing right now is unfolding your self-realization in the most amazing and unique way? Perhaps there isn't some special experience of self-realization that is the way to realize true nature. Maybe every soul's realization of true nature is meant to unfold in a completely unique way so that every soul's experience can also add to the experience of the One Being that all souls are a part of, just as every experience adds to the richness of your soul.

We resist this perspective when we really want self-realization to look a certain way. We want our realization to be like the dramatic experiences we read about in the biographies of the great masters and teachers. We use the fact that there are bigger experiences of self-realization to discount and reject the smaller experiences we are already having. And yet, the experiences we are having are also aspects of our Being. Everything from the most human thought or emotion to the most cosmic dimension of existence is an aspect of Being.

While there is freedom in experiencing a profound realization of an infinite dimension of our true nature, that freedom is only added to by an experience of a very human or limited dimension of that same true nature. Every experience adds to your soul, and no experience subtracts from your Being. This doesn't mean you don't discriminate between a small experience and a big one. Just as you can easily tell the difference between a teacup and a swimming pool, it is inherent in a small experience for it to feel small and for an infinite experience to feel infinite.

While the experience you are having right now while reading these words may or may not be the biggest realization of your life so far, it is the realization you are having right now. It will naturally feel big or small or somewhere in between. It will naturally have the specific qualities of this unique moment and not the qualities of any other experience. And yet, because it is happening right now, it is the most important realization you can have. In fact, it is the only realization you can have. It's too late or too soon to have any other experience than the one you are having right now, and this experience is making your soul richer and more fully realized than it was a moment ago.

Will you accept the precious gift the mystery is giving you right now?

why fear this moment
when no thoughts come
at last I lie naked
in the arms of experience

why fear this moment
when no words come
at last I find rest
in the lap of silence

why fear this moment
when love finds itself alone
at last I am embraced
by infinity itself

why fear this moment
when judgment falls away
at last my defenses
fail to keep intimacy at bay

why fear this moment
when hope is lost
at last my foolish dreams
are surrendered to perfection

HOW TO STAY FOCUSED ON THE SELF

Someone asked me about the teachings of Ramana Maharshi and how I stay focused on the Self. In my experience, the great power of Ramana's teaching is in the simplicity of the message. Self-inquiry points you all the way back to the source of Being in pure Presence. And yet, at times I also find that to be the limitation of this teaching. Formless awareness loves to play in form and in all of the many levels of existence—it even loves forming egos!

Perhaps, a balanced perspective is that there is a place for discovering your true nature as empty awareness, and yet, that isn't the end of the inquiry but only another beginning. There are all of the endless possibilities inherent in consciousness to be explored and enjoyed as well.

And so in answer to your question as to how I stay focused on the Self, I would say that as I discover more and more about the Self, I keep finding, in deeper ways, that there is nothing else here. That makes it easy to stay focused on the Self, as I can't miss it. Every experience is worthy of inquiry and deeper understanding and love.

KNOWING WHO YOU REALLY ARE

Self-realization is knowing who you really are. How do we know something? Is it enough to be told? Or is there something more that must happen for us to truly know something? Do we even need to be told who we already are? It would seem that the easiest thing in the world would be to know yourself. After all, you are right here. What could interfere with knowing this most intimate reality, your own self?

And yet from the very start, we were not told who we really are. Instead, were told something erroneous. We were told that who we are is the body, mind, and personality. Not only were we told this explicitly, but also reminded of it constantly by assumptions and implicit references to our body and mind as who we are. On top of that, we were reinforced for acting from our ego and personality. We were taught that good boys and girls don't do what comes naturally, but rather what their parents want them to do. So we formed a false identity to make our parents happy. This was necessary to get along and survive, and in the process, we developed the capacity to control ourselves and our actions.

However, at a certain point it is no longer necessary to have our actions controlled in this way. Our true nature is actually loving, wise, and careful. Even when our true nature acts spontaneously and a bit wildly, it is doing so in the context of its own great wisdom and perspective. So as we mature, our ego becomes a limitation and a distortion of our inherent wisdom and ability.

In the meantime, we have forgotten who we really are, so we come back to this question of knowing. How do you remember something you've forgotten? How can we recover a sense of the love and joy that is our innermost nature? While it helps to be told something, is that enough? For most of us, it takes something more than just being told. To really know something, it takes a direct experience of it and often a willingness to deeply sense and explore that experience. We must follow the words that describe our true nature to our actual sense of existing and then explore the mystery of the capacity to hear, think, feel, see, touch, ponder, and be aware that is present right now. The good news is that since what we are exploring is our own self, there is never any searching required. It is always right here wherever we are.

There is no formula for how much experience of our true nature is needed to realize an aspect of it or the whole truth of it. So we can only keep exploring, questioning, letting ourselves be pointed back to ourselves, and touching, listening, and sensing all that we can of the mystery of our own awareness and the pure empty space at its core. We are never done with this exploration. The truth of our nature is limitless, eternal, and always new. We are here to realize our true self, and it turns out that will only take forever. But what a way to spend eternity! Our being is an ever fresh, ever new dance between emptiness and form.

So while experience of our true nature is necessary to more fully realize it, no experience ever contains our true nature. The point of every spiritual experience is to make that experience irrelevant. A spiritual experience is like the envelope that our true nature is delivered in: It is totally necessary until you open it, and then it's useless. The point of any spiritual experience is simply to acquaint us with our true nature to the point that it doesn't matter anymore what we experience. Once we trust the source of our experience and know it as our own self, it no longer matters what we are experiencing. We can just go ahead and enjoy and explore our experience and our true nature for its own sake, not to gain anything and especially not to gain our self, because we are already here. There is nowhere to go and nothing to get. What a rich possibility it is to know that and then simply enjoy its ever new expression.

NOTHING HAPPENS TO YOU

Everything happens within you. Nothing happens to you. You are the consciousness that is experiencing the words on this page. That consciousness is so empty and spacious that nothing ever happens to it. Just as a thunderstorm passes through the sky but doesn't happen to the sky, every thought, feeling, desire, sensation, and event happens in awareness but not to it.

This truth is more obvious when it comes to an external event that doesn't take place near us. A bird flying high above us or the distant sound of traffic obviously happens within our field of awareness, but it doesn't feel like these events happen to us. But if that bird were to fly in front of our face or that traffic were to slow us down on the highway, it would feel like it was happening to us. Things that arise within our own body and mind feel even more like they happen to us. When a strong experience of fear, desire, or confusion arises, it seems like it's happening to us instead of within us.

The sky is unharmed by the thunderstorm, which is why we would say the storm happened *in* the sky instead of *to* the sky. What about your experiences, thoughts, feelings, and desires? Do they harm your awareness? Or do they eventually pass, like a summer raincloud? Is your awareness damaged by them, or is awareness still empty and awake, awaiting the next experience after a sensation, feeling, or thought passes?

Your body is within awareness. Because of its physical nature, something can happen to it that leaves a relatively lasting effect, but what about the awareness that is experiencing the body? Every sensation comes and goes in awareness. The sensations in your body are always changing, and your attention to them is always changing. Even pain is not in your awareness every moment. So even physical events or injuries don't happen to you but within you. What would it mean if a sore muscle or stomachache wasn't happening to you but only within your field of awareness? What if everything that happens within your body is just another event within the open sky of consciousness?

The most surprising thing is that this is even true of your innermost feelings and desires. Feelings of unworthiness and intense longings can arise within your chest or abdomen, which seem like part of you. But even they are happening within the field of awareness and not really to you. What would it mean if a deep feeling of sadness or an overwhelming desire for true love wasn't happening to you but just within your field of awareness? What if everything that moves within your heart and mind is just another event within the open sky of consciousness?

All experience passes like a raincloud and leaves behind the fresh, open space of endless awareness. The source of awareness is always here. You are always here. Everything else happens within awareness. Everything else comes and goes. There isn't even a separate you within awareness because you are the source of awareness. Nothing happens to you; everything happens within you.

YOU CANNOT BE HARMED

Consciousness is affected by experience but not harmed. It is the nature of aware consciousness to be affected by everything it experiences. Every color and sound, every event and experience, and every passing thought or feeling affects your consciousness. That is why we call it consciousness. A rock isn't as affected by these things, so we consider a rock less conscious than a person.

And yet, consciousness is not harmed by anything. That is its nature, that it can't be harmed. The form of anything can be harmed or permanently changed. Your body can be harmed, but the consciousness that contains your body cannot be harmed.

This is good news. It's like a "Get out of Jail" card in Monopoly. No matter what happens, you, as consciousness, are completely unharmed. What a relief! There is nothing that can harm you. No one and nothing has ever harmed you.

This is not to say that consciousness isn't affected deeply by both the good and bad things that happen to us. Every hurtful and unkind act leaves an impression in the consciousness of those involved. It's just that the impression doesn't permanently limit or damage the awareness of those involved. If something permanently affects us, it could be said to have harmed us. But if the effect is temporary, then what is the ultimate harm? Everything that profoundly affects our awareness, from the beautiful to the tragic, eventually passes. It is the miracle of our consciousness that it can heal from any wound, even if our body cannot.

What you are is eternal, aware space, or consciousness. You have a body, but you are not that body. So while your body can be permanently harmed, just like your car or camera can be, you as consciousness eventually heal or recover from every experience that has affected you. Even if the effect lasts for lifetimes, eventually it is diminished and disappears. From the perspective of something eternal, even many lifetimes isn't that long.

When you realize that your true nature as consciousness can't be harmed, that puts all of life's difficulties in perspective. Similarly, when someone's car is totaled in an accident but he or she isn't hurt, we consider that person lucky. This is because we have a perspective on the relative importance of damage to a car. It's not such a big deal relative to a serious physical injury or death. If you realize that you are aware space, then everything else is like the totaled car—no big deal.

Some things are still more important than others. Physical harm is still a bigger difficulty than harm to a car or other physical object. But by knowing that your true nature is space, which cannot be harmed, the bigger difficulties and even tragedies in life can be seen in perspective.

A simple question to ask is, "What effect does this experience have on my eternal soul?" And while everything leaves an impression on your awareness and your soul, nothing can ever permanently harm your soul, your true nature as empty awareness. In fact, every experience enriches your soul. Every moment adds to the depth and richness of your deepest knowing. We sense this in people who have faced a lot of difficulty in life and who have accepted their fate. There is a depth and wisdom that only comes from a wide range of experience, including painful and unwelcome experiences.

The willingness to meet and have any experience comes from the recognition that what you are is open, spacious awareness. Your body, mind, personality, emotions, and desires all appear within that awareness, but they are not you. And the real you cannot be harmed.

A LOVE POEM

Your hands have a cool dry touch
And yet they warm my heart
Your eyes are emptier than the night sky
And yet they pierce my defenses
Your body does not even exist
And yet you dance so beautifully
That I am lost in tears

How can silence say so much?
How can empty space feel so full?
Chasing after more and more is so futile
When only less will satisfy

WHY THINGS ARE THE WAY THEY ARE

Q: *Is there a reason for us being born with the gifts or limitations we have in life? Are they the result of karma from past lives? Are we given them as a cross to bear or as challenges meant to teach us specific lessons in life? Or is it just random—are we in these bodies for no reason beyond the fact that our parents didn't use contraception?*

A: Consciousness doesn't need a reason for things. It just loves experience, so it tries experiencing anything and everything it can. If it's true that our consciousness is limitless and eternal, then it makes a bit more sense that it would be willing to try anything. Eternity is a very long time. If you have eternity, then it makes sense that you would find lots of ways to pass the time. And by the way, the playful creation of experience also includes all the reasons you mention, such as karma, lessons to be learned, and also complete randomness of events. Again, consciousness has the time to try it every which way. So it tries out karma and evolution and learning. And then it also throws in lots of randomness just to keep itself on its toes!

PART 5

Awakening

WHAT IS ENLIGHTENMENT OR AWAKENING?

Just as the word love has been used to describe everything from a preference for ice cream to merging with everything, the words enlightenment and awakening are difficult to define because they've been used in so many different ways. They also are difficult to define because enlightenment and awakening are such ineffable and complex experiences.

Some definitions are very specific and narrow. One such definition for enlightenment is the complete dissolution of one's identity as a separate self with no trace of the egoic mind remaining. This sets the bar very high and means that very few people qualify as enlightened.

The opposite approach is to say that everyone is enlightened, that there is only awake consciousness. In this view, it's only a question of whether this natural awakeness has been recognized or not. Of course, when a word describes everything or everyone, it loses some of its usefulness. If everyone is enlightened, then why even talk about it?

Perhaps there's a definition that includes both of these perspectives, which recognizes that consciousness is always awake and enlightened, but the amount of awakeness, or aware consciousness, that is present in any moment can vary. This definition acknowledges that there's a difference in the amount of awakeness, or enlightened consciousness, that different people experience or that one person experiences at different times but still suggests that the potential for full awareness or becoming enlightened is the same for everybody. If every apparent individual consciousness is infinite in its potential, then each can also be infinite both in its capacity to expand or awaken and in its capacity to contract or identify with a narrow or limited experience.

If every consciousness is made of the same awareness and if everyone has an equal potential for enlightenment, then all expressions of consciousness are equally valid and valuable. Everyone truly is a Buddha or enlightened being, at least in potential. So defining enlightenment in many ways now makes sense, depending on what is being pointed to. One may use the word enlightenment to point to the state of self-realization beyond the ego or to point to the innate potential for this realization in all of us.

As for differentiating between the words enlightenment and awakening, *enlightenment* implies a more finished and constant state of realization, while *awakening* has more of the active quality of a verb and therefore suggests a movement or shift in consciousness. An awakening may be defined as a sudden increase in the overall amount of consciousness an individual is experiencing. There can be small awakenings and bigger awakenings. Not only does consciousness have unlimited potential for the amount of awakeness, but it also has an unlimited potential to shift in any way, at any moment. Consciousness can and sometimes does shift from contracted states of fear, anger, or hurt to expanded states of peace and joy in an instant. Unfortunately, it can also shift in the other direction. Consciousness has no fixed state.

As it is being defined here, a spiritual awakening is a sudden expansion or shift in consciousness, especially a more dramatic one (we don't usually refer to a minor realization as a spiritual awakening). Enlightenment, on the other hand can be used to mark a particular level of realization or awakeness, even if the exact definition varies depending on who is using the word, as it does with every word.

What really matters is what your awareness is doing right now. How is your consciousness appearing or shifting in this moment? Are you realizing more of your experience and Essence right now? Or are you contracting and limiting your awareness with thoughts and identification? Is any shifting happening from reading these words?

Enlightenment or awakening is a profound mystery, and the best definition may be found in the actual experience of your own shifts in consciousness. Just as it's more nourishing to eat an apple than read about one, so it can be more rewarding to explore the movements of your own awareness than to try to understand these things mentally. While definitions of such things can be helpful, it can also be beneficial to not have too many concepts, which could interfere with your actual experience. It's a good thing that language isn't so fixed or defined when it comes to spiritual unfoldment. Maybe the best definition of enlightenment is no definition. Then there is only what is found in your own direct experience of awareness.

THE FLOWER OF AWAKENING

Consider the miracle of a flower. What is it that causes a plant to flower? Does sunshine? Does lots of water? Or is it good soil? Maybe all of these together? Or is there really something more subtle in the nature of the flower itself that causes it to flower? Is it something in the DNA of the plant? Does that mean the whole process of evolution over eons of time is involved? What other factors might cause the flowering? Does gravity play a part? The season and the temperature? The quality of the light? What about animals that eat the fruit and spread the plant? Or the birds or bees that pollinate the flower? Do they cause the subsequent flowering of the newly established plants? Are there even subtler influences? What about Presence and love? The intention and attention of a gardener? And is the existence of the world of form itself necessary for a plant to flower? What about consciousness? Is there a force that directs the creation and unfolding of all form that is behind the appearance of a rose or a daisy?

What if what causes a flower is a combination of all of the things mentioned? And what if all of these things have to be in the right proportion? Is that proportion different for every species of plant? Some plants need lots of water or light to flower. Others will die with too much water or light. A unique formula is involved in the appearance of the simplest apple blossom and the most complex orchid.

When you consider all these influences and others that weren't mentioned or can't even be known or imagined, then it is truly a miracle when a flower appears. It's impossible to say what causes it to happen with any certainty or completeness. Yet, it's an act of incredible grace whenever all these diverse, subtle, and gross influences come together in just the right way for an iris or a daffodil to open its unique petals to the sky. If you trace all the factors back to all their causes, you find that everything that exists is somehow intimately connected to the cactus flower or dandelion in your front yard. We need a mysterious and powerful word like "grace" to name this amazing interplay of forces and intelligence. To reduce it to a formula doesn't come close to capturing or describing the vast richness of variables and forces at play. There's no formula complex enough to capture the mystery of a magnolia blossom.

Awakening is a kind of flowering of consciousness. When consciousness expands and opens into a new expression, we call that an awakening. And while there are as many kinds of awakenings as there are flowers, they are all equally mysterious. What is it that causes a child to awaken to the nature of words and language? How does one suddenly know he or she is falling in love? And how does one explain the birth of unconditional or divine love?

What are the causes of the most profound spiritual awakenings, where consciousness suddenly recognizes its true nature? Why does that type of flowering appear in one consciousness today and another one tomorrow? If the formula for a simple petunia is a vastly complex interplay of earthly, human, and even cosmic forces, then imagine how complex the formula is for the unfolding of a human consciousness into full awakeness. The good news is that we can't and don't need to know the totality of the formula for growing petunias, and we can't and don't need to know the formula for spiritual realization. Yet, we can be curious about all the factors involved and even play with them to see what effects, if any, they may have in our own experience of consciousness unfolding.

Sometimes the mysteriousness and unpredictability of the

process of awakening leads us to conclude it is all up to grace or God. And, of course, that is true. But does that mean there's no place in this unfolding for our own actions? Is there a place for spiritual practice? What about meditation, self-inquiry, or studying spiritual texts? What about devotional practices or the transmission of Presence from a great teacher or master? We can easily become disillusioned with these activities because the results can be so unpredictable and varied, and it may seem simpler to avoid the question of their role altogether. Ask any gardener if it works every time to water, weed, and fertilize a plant? Or does a plant sometimes fail to flower no matter how well it is cared for? However, does that mean you never water or fertilize your plants?

At other times, we can be overly convinced that our practice or inquiry will produce the desired results, maybe because it worked for us once or for someone we know. The only problem with spiritual practices is that they occasionally work! Then we think we have the formula and that every time we meditate or ask, "Who am I?" we'll have the same experience of expansion or Oneness. That's like thinking you'll have a bumper crop of marigolds every time you plant them.

There is a middle way between denying the value of spiritual practice and expecting that inquiry, meditation, or devotional practice will, by itself, result in awakening. We can experiment and play with these practices, just as a gardener experiments with different fertilizers or watering patterns. In the end, it is all up to grace. But what if grace works through us as well as on us? What if spiritual practice is as much a part of the mystery of existence as anything else?

Maybe we can hold the question of what role inquiry, devotion, effort, surrender, transmission, meditation, gratitude, intention, silencing the mind, studying spiritual books, involvement with a teacher or master, ripeness of the student, karma, grace, and luck play in our awakening with an openness and curiosity instead of needing to define their roles once and for all. The flowering of your consciousness is as unique as every flower, and you are here to discover how it's going to happen uniquely through you.

What is your consciousness like right now? How open is the flower of your awareness? Is it still budding, or has it blossomed? Just as every flower fades and another comes along, what about now? And now? What happens this time when you meditate? What happens now when you inquire, "Who am I?" How does it feel right now to open your heart with gratitude even if nothing much is happening? What impact does reading this or anything else have on you? Every stage of a plant's existence is valuable and even necessary for its flowering. Your experience is always adding to the richness of the unfolding of your consciousness in this moment. May you enjoy the garden of your true nature.

BURNING DOWN THE HOUSE

Q: *I've come to believe (aside from the grace that some people experience, where their whole world crumbles and reveals what's beyond the individual personality, the abiding nondual awareness) that one has to ignite one's own world on fire in order to awaken. Can you recommend any way of igniting this whole thing? I don't seem to have the existential crisis that so many of the masters I respect have had.*

A: My own sense is that there really is no formula for spiritual awakening. Some people experience a kind of crumbling of their world that leads to a deeper opening, while others experience a graceful and easeful unfolding into the depths of their Being. And of course, some people whose lives crumble are only traumatized by that experience, not awakened, and some who experience a lot of ease and comfort never question very deeply.

So in answer to your question about how to ignite a burning, I would suggest a more general approach of being very curious and accepting of whatever is arising. Often when we try to ignite things or, on the other hand, try to stop the crumbling or burning, we only interfere with the deeper intelligence that actually knows the way things need to go. But by being curious and present to whatever is happening, you allow the process of awakening to unfold in the most natural way for you.

This means being very curious and aware when a burning or crumbling or any kind of difficulty or challenge arises. But it's equally fruitful to be intensely curious about the easy and fun moments, when life unfolds abundantly and delightfully. And finally, you can inquire into and explore the ordinary moments, when life is maybe a little boring or predictable.

This attitude of gently touching experience as it is already happening means that when a burning desire for the truth does arise, you have developed the capacity to stay with that experience all of the way. However it's not your job to set the whole house on fire. Fortunately, every experience has the same potential to be a doorway into the depths of your Being. Why miss all the richness and many flavors of Being that are presenting themselves when life is easy or ordinary?

WANTING TO AWAKEN

Q: *What can I do about the impatience to wake up now?*

A: If you truly want to wake up, then I invite you to get very curious about the awakeness that is here right now. Are you aware of anything at all in this moment? What is that awareness like? Just as a single drop of water is wet, the awareness that is reading these words has all the qualities of your true nature. Does the part of you that is already aware and awake need to wake up, or is it already profoundly and mysteriously aware? Just for a moment, instead of seeking more awareness, find out more about the awareness that's already here.

The awareness that's here in this moment is alive, spacious, discriminating, and full of love. Everything that really matters is found in this awareness. Love, peace, and joy flow from within us out to the experiences we have of the world. Seeking the source of peace or love in the world is like looking for the source of the water in the puddle that forms under a water faucet. Not only is the source here within us, but it's also flowing right now as the simple awareness that is reading these words.

SEEKING, GIVING, AND BEING

The spiritual life can be divided into three stages: seeking or acquiring, giving or expressing, and being. Each of these three stages has unique characteristics and qualities, and each is equally important and necessary. They are not linear, but rather a cycle that moves from one to the next and back again.

The first stage of seeking is a period of searching for truth and trying to get there. It's the period of greatest doing and also the greatest sense of a separate self that is seeking. This is what most of the world is up to, although most people are seeking or acquiring wealth and fame and the other things the ego wants. But underlying even these activities is a deeper pull to find love, peace, and happiness. The ego just mistakenly thinks money or fame will give it peace, love, and happiness. Eventually, the individual discovers that these ego-driven activities don't really satisfy, so the seeking becomes more subtle and direct. We eventually seek peace itself and love itself, not something that will bring us peace or love.

The second stage, giving or expressing, is what naturally happens when we start finding true love and happiness. It's such a joy to find the real sources of satisfaction and fulfillment that we are inspired to share love and joy with others and to express them in everything we do. This phase is still a phase of doing, but there's much less of a sense of a separate self that is doing it. It seems more like we are being done by the love and joy flowing through us.

The third stage, being, is really a moving beyond the duality of the first two stages into a place of such complete fullness and perfection that there's no more need or pull to do anything. There's a simple recognition that you already are everything and so is everybody else. So what need is there to seek or find, or give or express? Everything is already fulfilled beyond any possibility of improvement or gain. Outwardly, this is a time of very little doing beyond taking care of the basic necessities of life. There's no motivation to do anything for what it will accomplish or give you, so it's enough most of the time to just rest and be.

The first thing we tend to do when we hear about these stages is to try to apply them as a prescription for our spiritual life. We try to do the actions of the second and especially the third stages as a way to get there. And yet, these stages aren't a prescription, but simply a description of the phases or cycles of our spiritual life. They are a description of how Essence, or Being, moves in this world of form. In fact, to try to get to the second or third stage is really an expression of the first stage. It's trying to achieve or acquire spiritual depth.

Instead, we can simply be curious about how these stages are unfolding in our life. They are all necessary aspects of spiritual life, and one isn't better than the other. Each phase can naturally follow the others in an endless cycle of movement from pure being to active creation and doing and back again.

It's not uncommon to overemphasize one of these stages or to become stuck or attached to any point in the cycle. Most of us have experienced being stuck in the first phase and being very attached to achieving and acquiring more happiness and spiritual realization. In the process of seeking these, we often become attached to the activity of seeking itself because it gives us a sense of a mission and purpose. Being a spiritual seeker is quite a dramatic and inspiring thing.

We can become just as stuck in the second phase, in the identity as someone who has found the truth and is now here to give it to others. The sense of identity that comes from being a spiritual teacher or guide is quite seductive. While it's natural and fulfilling to be a teacher or guide once you've discovered the truth, there's no lasting identity to be found in this, and any attempt to form an identity around being a spiritual teacher will eventually become a source of suffering.

One can't really speak of getting stuck in the third stage, as it isn't a place where any identity can form or any attachment can happen. There's only everything being as it is and no sense of a separate self to be stuck. However, as the cycle repeats and we find ourselves back in a phase of doing or giving, we may then form an attachment to our memory of the pure state of being that we seem to have lost.

EFFORT IN MEDITATION

Someone emailed me with some questions about the role of effort in meditation, and about their tendency to try to hard until they felt a sense of strain while meditating. Here is my response:

It seems to come down to the question of effort or no effort. And yet there is an in-between place, where you make the minimum amount of effort. That is what meditation is really for: to find the place where you are efforting the very least amount possible. The very least amount of effort is to just notice what is happening and then allow it to be the way it is.

This does require effort, but so little effort that the tendency is to still try too hard, for example by focusing the noticing in some way, like noticing the thoughts. More simply, you can just notice whatever awareness touches, whether it is a thought, a sensation, a blank or empty experience, or even an arising of Presence.

The point of this minimal effort is to simply to be present. The only measure of whether it was a "good" meditation or not is whether you sat there for the allotted time or not. Anything else that happens or any results of the meditation are not your concern. Even surrender is not something you do, it is just something that happens to you. By meditating, you are present if surrender happens to you. You are also present if conditioning gets triggered or dissolution of the ego and merging into the Absolute happens. You are also present if your butt starts to ache or you get restless. You are present if nothing happens. Your only job is to be present. Everything else is in the hands of Being, or Presence, not in your hands.

However, there is a little twist to all of this in that if trying too hard arises, then you can just be present to the experience of trying too hard. You mention a feeling of strain that arises. What is that like? How do you know there is strain? What sensations are present that let you know there is strain present? Are they bad sensations? You don't need to fix or change the experience of straining; just give it attention like anything else.

There are practical things you can do to allow yourself to be more present. One of them is to drop into the Heart, or you may also try dropping your awareness all the way down into your belly. Then just let the noticing happen from the Heart or belly. This accesses the natural capacity of your Being to just notice.

Lastly, you can simply know that everything is working perfectly. The actual unfolding and awakening of your consciousness is not something you do. It's just something that happens to you. Meditation and even self-inquiry are just a means to be home when Presence arises. They don't cause Presence to happen, they just mean that you are noticing when it does happen.

SITTING ON A BEACH DOESN'T CAUSE A TSUNAMI

Q: *I would like to know your thoughts on the importance (or not) of meditation in general.*

A: Meditation can be helpful, but meditation itself doesn't cause the deeper shifts of awareness that just happen as a result of divine grace. My sense is that most spiritual practices function to focus our awareness on the here and now. That doesn't cause a shift in consciousness to happen necessarily, but it does mean that when a shift happens, you are there to notice more about it.

I recently used the metaphor that sitting on the beach doesn't cause a tsunami, but it does mean that when a tsunami comes, you are there to be swept away by it. Of course a tsunami might still get you even if you aren't near the beach, but the odds are better at the beach.

So meditation and other spiritual practices are like spending time at the beach. They don't cause any big waves of awakening, but they might mean that you are swept up when those waves occur. This puts the practice in perspective. You don't measure a spiritual practice by its results; you measure it by whether or not you actually sit and meditate today. If nothing happens today, that's fine. You just come back to the beach again tomorrow.

You can enjoy the sun, sand, and sound of the ocean while you are there, but the real purpose is just to be here when the deeper movements of Being happen. This is true of the tsunami-like awakenings and also the smaller rogue waves that come and wash away your attachments and suffering a little at a time.

FOCUS IN MEDITATION

Q: *I have to admit that I often find myself not wanting to do the practice, not wanting to do the inner work to feel whatever pain may be there. Another thing is that I find it so incredibly difficult to focus. I realize that this seemingly lack of focus might stem from not wanting to feel whatever needs to be felt or to think deeply about my life and take actions in a responsible way.*

A: I would offer two seemingly opposite, but actually complementary, suggestions for the arising of resistance or a reluctance to do the work and also for your lack of focus. The first suggestion, when there is resistance or a lack of focus, is to just try harder. Keep bringing yourself back to the practice or object of your focus, whether it is a meditative practice or a form of inquiry or inner work. If a distraction comes up, notice it and then bring yourself back to whatever you are focusing on or to your inner process. Having to bring yourself back again and again to your point of focus builds a spiritual muscle, so to speak, which will eventually make it easier to stay with the practice or the process longer and longer. However, just as you can never lift a heavy weight forever, you will never reach a point where you can focus indefinitely.

The other suggestion is to explore the distractions. If a resistance or reluctance to look within arises, then become curious about that. What's it like to not want to do the work? How do you know you don't want to do it? Is there a feeling in your body? Is there something you say to yourself or picture in your mind? If you had to teach me how to resist the process, how would you teach me to do that?

Similarly, if you can't focus on something even after you've tried, then focus on the experience of not being able to focus. What's that like? Where does your attention go instead? Can you focus on not wanting to focus? Can you focus on the distractions that come up? What is the urge to do something else like? How do you even know if you are focusing or not?

You will find that you can focus easily if you just let yourself focus on whatever is actually arising in this moment. Instead of trying to focus on a meditation or task, just let yourself be present to your daydreams, feelings, restlessness, discouragement, confusion, desire, or whatever is appearing in your awareness right now, without getting lost in those thoughts or feelings; just notice them as they appear. So if you can't stay focused on a particular experience, just let your awareness and curiosity fully explore the experience you are having.

This second approach is more like stretching a muscle rather than strengthening a muscle. When stretching a muscle, you relax and allow the muscle to open and expand. It doesn't work to push or strain to try to stretch the muscle. Sometimes it's okay to stretch by letting your awareness move however it moves. Make it your practice to be curious about your distractions whenever your effort to focus fails.

These two approaches are exactly opposite: In one you push with the maximum amount of effort, and in the other you exert as little effort as possible by simply directing your awareness to where it already is. By using both of these approaches, you'll develop the greatest strength, range, and flexibility of awareness possible. But that isn't really the goal because your awareness already has limitless strength and flexibility. What you discover is that your awareness is already fine just the way it is, and it has always been perfectly fine. This is the simple realization that all of your effort is in service to. By using this "muscle" called awareness in every way possible, you eventually realize the perfect nature of awareness itself. It isn't what you can do with awareness that matters, but the recognition that awareness is already perfect, and that awareness is what you really are.

PART 6

Doing and Choosing

WHAT DO I DO WHEN THERE IS NO DOER?

Spiritual teachings suggest that there is no doer, that there is no separate self that is the source of our actions. This teaching often causes a lot confusion, as it is contrary to our experience. It seems that there is a doer and that *I* am the doer: *I* get up in the morning, *I* walk the dog, and *I* drive to work. How do these things happen if there is no doer? And if there is no doer, then what do I do? How do I live my life if there is no one here to live it? What do I do if there is no doer?

This confusion exists because spiritual teachings point to something that doesn't exist in the usual way. The nature of reality can't be described or explained with words, and it can't be experienced through the ordinary senses. In speaking about something that can't be spoken about, the easiest approach is often to use negation. If you can't speak directly about something, then you're left with saying what it is not.

So spiritual teachings contain a lot of negation: There is no self. There is no doer. The world is an illusion. Not this. Not that. Negation can be effective in pointing us away from illusions, such as the idea of *me*, and other false and mistaken ideas. If you take a moment to look for yourself, you discover that there is no individual self, only an idea of a self. The "I" is just an idea. So in this sense, it is accurate to say that there is no self and no doer.

However, the mind can't conceive of or even really experience nothing. If you are experiencing something, then that is by definition not nothing. So when the mind is pointed to nothing or to the absence of a self or a doer, it makes a picture or concept of nothing and thinks about that. If we are told there is no doer, the mind makes a picture of the absence of somebody, something like an empty chair or a broom sweeping by itself.

Again, this contradicts our actual experience: There is something in the chair when I sit down in it. The broom only sweeps when I pick it up and start sweeping. So there is obviously a distortion or inaccuracy in the approach of negation. While negation does evoke a certain experience of emptiness that can be spacious and restful, it doesn't capture the totality of reality. It leaves out our actual experience of the real world.

Another approach is the opposite: Instead of saying there is no self, there is no world, and there is no doer, we can say there is only Self, the world is all one thing, and it is this totality of existence that does everything. In other words, *everything* sweeps the floor and sits in the chair. If we look deeply into our experience, we can see that there is some truth to this perspective. If we trace back all of the causes of any action, we see that there are an infinite number of influences or causes for the simplest action.

For example, you may sweep the floor because your mother taught you to keep a spotless house and your dad taught you to be responsible, not to mention all the other messages you received from the culture and society about cleanliness and responsibility. Add to that all the people that influenced your mom and dad and everyone else who ever had an impact on you. And what about all the factors that led to the particular path of evolution that gave you those opposable thumbs that allow you to use a broom? If you include all the factors at play when you pick up a broom and sweep, you can see how it might make sense to say that everyone and everything is sweeping the floor. There is a doer, but it isn't you; it is everything. And by the way, all of these factors are at work if you don't sweep the floor. Not doing something is just another thing we do.

This approach of including more and more instead of negating everything is also a useful teaching tool. It evokes a sense of the oneness and richness of life. But again, it doesn't capture the actual experience of an action like sweeping. If only *everything* would sweep my floor, then *I* could go take a nap. Speaking about everything as the doer of everything that is done also doesn't capture the sense of no self that is experienced when we look within using spiritual practices such as self-inquiry.

So if it isn't complete to say that there is no doer, and if it isn't complete to say that everything is the doer, what's wrong with just saying that *I* sweep the floor, and be done with it? For purely practical purposes, saying "I" do something is enough. But as already noted, saying "I" leaves out the many rich and complex causes of our actions, and it leaves out the absence of a separate self that we discover when we look within. It also doesn't suggest that there's more to this reality than meets the eye.

So we are left with a dilemma: It's incomplete to say that there is no doer, it's incomplete to say that everything is the doer, and it's incomplete to say that I am the doer. It's like a multiple choice test where all of the answers are wrong! Yet, what is it like to not have an answer? What's it like to hold the question even when you've exhausted all of the possible answers?

The question of what is going on here, what is this experience of doing, can be a rich experience in and of itself. Such a question can put us more in touch with our experience than any answer can. The question invites a direct sensing of the various levels of our experience. As the broom moves across the floor, is it possible to simultaneously experience the emptiness within, the richness of the oneness of all things, and the personal actions of our particular body? Why do we have to choose one?

And what about the original question, "What do I do?" Could this also be a rich opportunity to explore all the dimensions of existence? Why does there have to be a right answer? Can the question, itself, evoke a deeper sensing of life and an endless willingness to question again and again? What do I do now? And what about now? The gift may be in the question itself, not in some final answer. Life is unfolding in ever new and different ways, so maybe only in each new moment can we discover what the *everything and nothing* that we are is going to do next.

There is an assumption that spiritual teachings are supposed to bring us spiritual answers, that we are supposed to finally get somewhere. But what if the point of this spiritual journey is the journey itself? What if the answers are true and relevant when they arise, but they become irrelevant in the next breath? So perhaps the question of what to do isn't meant to ever be done with or fully answered. Letting go of the idea of a right or final answer can make the question come alive in this very moment. What are you doing right now? What is most true to do now? And then, what about now? It's always time to ask again because it's always a new now.

Just for this moment, find out what happens if you just allow yourself to not know what the right thing to do is, who would do it, and even if there is anything to do, or if doing even really happens. When you question that deeply, is there more or less of a compulsion to act in unhealthy or ignorant ways? Or is there a natural curiosity and sense of wonder that arises and puts you very much in touch with all of the mysterious elements that make up this particular moment? Does this curiosity lead you to rash and silly decisions, or does it allow impulses and intuitions to arise from a deeper place within your being? If you know less and less about doing, what happens next?

The gift of the deepest spiritual questions arises in the day-to-day living of life. Asking, "What do I do?" can lead you on an exploration that has no boundaries, and the journey can only start here and now. What most often limits us is our conclusions. The simple antidote is to ask another question: "What do I do when there is no doer, when everything is the doer, and when it's also up to me to do something?"

WHAT ABOUT FREE WILL?

Q: Nonduality seems to be a repudiation of free will: I'm not doing anything; the divine acts through me. But what about the man who murders a child, or genocidal wars? It seems the world would often be better if people acted differently. Can you help me understand this?

A: This is one of the most common concerns raised about the teachings of nonduality. While there is just one Being here, the manifestations and movements of that one Being are as diverse as can be. Oneness seems to love to appear and dance as many. And there are also many levels of truth that operate within this amazing dance of life. So your question about murder and war can be answered at different levels, and all of the answers would have some relevance. At the most relative level—the level of ordinary consciousness—there appears to be free will. From this perspective, it is important what we do, and if people made better choices, this would be wonderful for the world.

If we shift to a more absolute perspective—the perspective of Oneness, where all is known to be happening within one Being—we realize that everything that happens is a projection of this one consciousness, and nothing that has happened has harmed consciousness, not even murder and war.

We can experience how both of these perspectives are true, and it is also possible to experience a perspective that is in between these two extremes. When someone has a profound realization of their true nature, this doesn't necessarily lead to a disinterest in this world. In fact, the recognition that there is no separate self usually leads to the experience and expression of a deep love for this world. Once we see that the false self is illusory, we lose any motivation for murder or war.

Once the false self has been seen through, we aren't left with nothing. When the ego's grip has been loosened, the qualities of our true nature are revealed: love, joy, peace, clarity, strength, and wisdom. At our core, we are loving, joyful, and divine. This isn't something we can grasp intellectually, but it is something we experience as our sense of self is weakened or dissolved through spiritual inquiry.

Many have an intellectual grasp of the concept that there is no individual doer and that the world is just an illusion. When this is only grasped intellectually and not experientially, such a belief can lead to all kinds of distortions and justifications for terrible actions. For examples, just examine the history of religious fundamentalism, where teachings about peace and love have been used to justify hatred, murder, and war. Even a belief in there being no doer can lead to this kind of fundamentalism if it is just a belief.

On the other hand, an actual experience of the ego dissolving results in an opening up to the deeper reality of our Being, which cannot be described or defined. At that depth of experience, it is seen that only goodness exists and that no opposite thing called badness exists. It is this core of goodness that loves the world and everything in it and makes it unlikely that someone resting in Essence would ever purposely harm another. Instead, there is a natural arising of compassion and an appreciation for all of life.

The concept of nonduality is just that—a concept. As such, it can be distorted and co-opted by the ego and the mind to justify anything. But the reality of our nondual nature is not a concept, and the direct experience of it is filled with peace, love, and joy beyond anything we could have imagined. But don't take my word for any of this. See what you find when you inquire deeply into this question of who it is that acts in this world. Do you find a lack of love and concern for the world when you experience your true nature, or do you find that there's no limit to the love and compassion that can be found within the empty spaces of your soul?

LIVING AS NO SELF

Q: *How can I keep the perspective of there being no separate self in the midst of the practical demands of daily life, and how can I live more fully from that perspective?*

A: The truth is there is no separate self, and it is also true that functioning as an apparent separate self is necessary. These are not contradictory truths, but complementary truths. Often in spiritual teachings there is an emphasis on the nondual truth (there is no separate self), since most people haven't realized this truth yet. But before, during, and after realizing this truth, you still have to function in the world.

Once you recognize this truth, the practical considerations, such as getting along with your boss and taking care of your family, don't disappear, but you can hold them more lightly. And it is possible to recognize more clearly that there is a deeper Presence unfolding all of life and that it knows what you need to do and not do to take care of yourself and others in a practical way.

***

Q: *Because the "I" is just a thought, how can a thought make a decision or take an action?*

A: You point out that the "I" thought is just a thought and therefore can't do anything, but what about that which thinks the "I" thought? What is that? Can it act? In the Diamond Approach, which I've been studying for several years, there is a realization of the unreality of the ego, or self-image, but there is also a recognition of a truer individual self that is a unique expression of the Oneness as it is incarnate in a particular person. In many spiritual traditions this is referred to as the "pearl beyond price," as it can have a pearl-like quality when it is experienced. It has a solidity and reality that is way beyond the experience of the ego.

Just as an experiment, reach up and tap the top of your head. The *you* that can make choices and take action is the same *you* that just tapped your head. Ultimately, everything, including you, is an illusion, but within the illusion you have choice and free will.

Life will unfold according to the will of the divine. If you leave out this bigger truth, you'll suffer from thinking it is all up to you, which is a set up for either a sense of failure or a sense of false pride. However, if you leave out the smaller truth that you still need to choose and act, then you'll suffer as a result of thinking that there's nothing you can do. If this incomplete view is taken all of the way to its logical conclusion, then there's no one to ever do anything, and you might as well just stay where you are right now and starve to death. But even then, you haven't escaped the smaller truth, since you'll find that you have to choose to keep sitting there, even as you get hungrier and hungrier.

The balanced view is to leave everything up to God, except what is right in front of you to do in this moment. If you are hungry, eat. If you are tired, sleep. If you are sick, find a way to heal. If there's a choice to be made, check what is truest to do and then do it. Then you can forget about the results of your actions because that part isn't up to you. That part is up to the bigger truth of God's will. There is a line in the *Tao Te Ching*: "Do your work and then step back." This reminds us that our actions are up to us, but the results of our actions are not up to us.

WHAT MOVES LIFE

There is an innate wisdom unfolding this life, and it always gets you where you need to go. It seems that what is unfolding life also loves to play and create so much that it even gives you the power to choose and act as an apparent individual. So the ego, or false self, makes choices, and those choices often take life and awareness in directions that cause us to suffer. The ego wants to create what it wants regardless of what Being wants! There's no mistake in all of this. The Oneness loves the unpredictable ego that it has created!

At times, the ego's desires move us, and at other times, we are moved by deeper drives coming from Essence, which is a truer aspect of our individuality than the ego that moves in harmony with the wisdom of Being. We may also recognize an even deeper source of everything and surrender to that: We can, paradoxically, choose what is being chosen by Being for us in every moment. We can say yes to life as it is unfolding before us.

There is quite a dance going on between the ego, Essence, and Being that allows Being to create unpredictability and surprise within itself. Maybe that's the only way that something that is already infinite and eternal can create and play—by allowing something new and unpredictable to be created within itself.

***

Q: *The greatest love, peace, and joy I've experienced in life came from believing everyday life had been predetermined before I was born. In other words, I had no power to change anything. I was simply watching life unfold moment by moment. Life was wonderful. This was years ago. Now that I feel I'm in control, I'm very lost.*

A: I would suggest that both perspectives are true, but the perspective of everything being predetermined is the bigger truth, although I tend to think of it not as predetermined, but rather determined by the infinite intelligence of Being, which appears predetermined from our limited perspective.

In the more limited perspective of our everyday life, it seems like we are in control or at least choosing what we do. Within the realm of our daily life, it is even important to choose and learn, grow and evolve the very best we can. We must act as if our choices matter, because at this level they do matter.

At the same time, a larger intelligence is unfolding life perfectly according to a divine plan that we can sense or intuit but can't really comprehend or know ahead of time. This divine intelligence that breathes our body, also grows the trees, arranges the stars and galaxies, and brings us the experiences we are meant to be having.

So both are true: We must make choices, *and* everything is happening according to a plan. You could say that our choices are part of the divine plan.

There's another dimension to all of this, and that is the potential to simply choose what is already so. When we do this, the two dimensions meet. We surrender our power to choose to the limitless intelligence of Being. In a sense, all spiritual practices, whether it is a form of meditation, inquiring into who you really are, or being present, are a form of choosing what already is. In every case, there is an invitation to surrender the effort to change what is and simply sense or inquire into what already is so.

This place where choice meets the deeper truth is very fertile ground for an infusion of insight and understanding into our awareness. It isn't that a spiritual practice makes anything happen, but it does put us in the most likely place for something profound to happen, including something as simple as noticing how beautiful and mysterious the moment-to-moment unfolding of life really is.

PART 7

Beyond No Self

The spiritual journey is a movement away from over-identification with the body and mind to the rediscovery of our true identity as infinite Being, and this can be two different movements. The first movement is dis-identification with the body and mind. Since identification is just a movement of thought, dis-identification is simply a movement away from thought. The ego identification that we experience most of the time is the result of repeated thoughts about "I," "me," and "mine." That is all there is to it, but while we are thinking these thoughts the sense of self is contained in them. And since most of our self-referencing thoughts are about our body, our thoughts, our feelings, and our desires, the sense of self is usually contained in the body and mind.

Dis-identification from the thought form of the ego can occur whenever there is a deep questioning of the assumption that is present in most of our thoughts that we are the body and the mind. Inquiry using the question, "Who am I?" can naturally weaken the assumption that we are the body and the mind. In fact, any deep questioning of our thoughts and assumptions can loosen our over-identification with thought, since so many of our thoughts aren't very true. Experiences of no thought can also weaken this identification because in the absence of thought, is an absence of identification. We all experience this when we get so caught up in what we are doing that we completely "forget ourselves."

Alternatively, sensing the Presence that is aware of the thoughts can also disentangle us from the tendency to identify with our thoughts. The second movement of the spiritual journey is this recognition, or realization, of our true nature as Presence, or limitless Awareness. It is a wonderful surprise to discover that everything that really matters in life, including peace, joy, and love, is found in this empty Awareness. This emptiness is incredibly full and rich. It has intelligence, strength, and compassion. Whenever we experience a deeper quality of Being, such as clarity, peace, insight, value, happiness, or love, it's coming from this spacious Presence.

The surprising thing is that while these two movements can occur simultaneously, they can also happen apart from each other. When this happens, the movement from ego identification to our essential nature is incomplete. Although it's a profound insight and a huge relief to discover, by examining and questioning our thoughts, that we are not the body or the mind (after all, if I'm not my body, then these aren't my aches and pains; and if I'm not my mind, then these aren't my problems), by itself this insight only reveals our false assumptions, not the truth about who we really are. So it's possible to dissolve the ego by seeing through the mind without actually experiencing our true nature, which is a Heart-centered experience. In a sense, you can wake up out of your mind but not be in your Heart.

When this happens, there is a sense of relief from all the grief caused by over-identification with the body and mind but also often a deep sense of meaninglessness: If *I* don't exist, then what's the point? It doesn't matter anymore what the fictional *I* does or what happens to it. In fact, it feels like nothing matters at all because everything is so clearly an illusion.

When seekers are led or just find their own way to a deep experience of no self, they can then form a new, more subtle belief that this absence of self is all there is. "I'm not my body, I'm not my mind, I don't exist" are seen as the final conclusions. From a purely logical perspective, what more is there to say, since there's no one here to say it or hear it! And while these conclusions are true, they aren't the *whole* truth.

Underlying all the mind's activity is the non-conceptual reality of Being, or our true nature. It is a pure, empty, aware space that is full of the subtle substance of Presence and all of its essential qualities: peace, joy, love, clarity, strength, value, and much more. How can that be—empty space that is full of everything that matters? The mind can't grasp it fully, as Presence exists beyond concepts. And yet, that is what we really are. We experience it with more subtle senses than the physical senses and the mind. We "sense" it by being it. We just are this full, yet empty, Presence.

It is this second movement of realization of Presence that counteracts the belief that since I (as ego) don't exist, therefore nothing exists and everything is an illusion. The realization of Presence, or Essence, gives back to our life a heartfelt sense of meaning and purpose, which becomes a pure expression of the wonder and beauty of this deeper reality. Instead of living a life in service to the ego's wants and needs, we are moved to fulfill the deepest purpose of a human life: to serve and express freedom, joy, beauty, peace and love. By itself, the realization of no self can end up dry and lifeless, but when the Heart opens wide to the greater truth of the true Self, life is anything but dry and lifeless.

The opposite can also occur: Our awareness can move into pure Presence and be filled with a sense of the limitless goodness of our true nature. And while any experience of our true nature does, to some extent, loosen the identification with the limited idea of ourselves that we call the ego, an experience of our true nature by itself doesn't always dissolve the ego completely. Having a profound experience of our true nature doesn't take away our capacity to identify. It doesn't render us incapable of thought. We can still return to thinking of ourselves as a limited self—but one that has now tasted our true nature.

So, after such an experience, if the habit of identification with the body and mind does continue, it may still be necessary to deconstruct the mistaken beliefs related to ego identification. There's a place for inquiring into the false beliefs and assumptions of our identification with the body and mind, and a place for inquiring into the underlying reality. The difference is that inquiry into our true nature isn't a purely mental activity. Because of the subtle nature of Presence, the inquiry has to be subtle and wholehearted. To discover what's really here requires subtlety, patience, persistence, courage, tenderness, compassion, curiosity, and ultimately everything you've got! The momentum of our usual identification with thoughts and physical reality shapes our perception to such a great degree that breaking through to the more subtle dimensions of perception can be a challenge.

It helps to pursue the inquiry into true nature with both the Heart and the body. The mind's view is so easily distorted by belief and conditioning that the experience beneath the shoulders is often a more direct and open doorway into Presence. What are you experiencing right now in your shoulders? In your heart? In your belly? What is the space around your arms and legs like right now? Is there energy flowing in your body right now? Questions like these can direct you to a more fruitful exploration, especially if you ask them with your whole being and not just with your mind.

It is a saving grace that this deeper reality is always present. Sometimes it only touches us in an unguarded moment of deep loss or profound beauty. In the end, there's no escaping from the truth. Illusions come and go, beliefs come and go, but the underlying Presence remains.

To experience Presence, all we have to do is stop believing in our thoughts and sense our being. It is really that simple, although doing this isn't necessarily easy. One of the things that makes experiencing Presence a challenge is the sense of identity we naturally have. Anytime we add something to the statement "I am," as in "I am scared" or "I am a bird watcher," our identity moves into that thought. This is what it means to identify with thought. A thought by itself has little power or significance. But a thought that begins with "I" or "I am" or one that is about me, my possessions, or my experience evokes a sense of identity. It's as if our true nature moves into or tries on the shape and feel of the thought. Dissolving or deconstructing the thoughts that we identify with can free our essential identity from an assumption that it is somehow contained in our body or our mind. Seeing the falseness of those ideas opens the door for our deepest sense of our own existence to move out of the tight confines of our beliefs and ego identifications.

Often when the sense of self is set free from the structures of ego-centered thought, it naturally expands into a full experience of true nature. We call a sudden expansion into true nature like this an awakening, as it seems we have awakened to a whole new reality that is rich and full of joy, peace, and love.

However, then it is possible for the sense of self, or identity, to move into a different belief or an assumption of no self. This happens most often when the focus of a teaching or inquiry is on the negation of false identifications, without a counter-balancing emphasis on the underlying reality of Presence. Some spiritual practices are specifically designed to negate false identifications, such as the practice of seeing that you are not this and not that until nothing is left. Some spiritual teachers and teachings emphasize the non-existence of a separate individual and go on to suggest that not only is the individual not real, but the world and everything in it is also not real.

There is a profound truth in this perspective, as it penetrates and dissolves the usual belief or assumption that the ego, our thoughts, and physical reality are more real than more subtle levels of reality. Even when we have tasted a deeper reality, we often return to an ego-centered perspective because of the momentum of our involvement with the physical and mental realms. Even in the face of profound experiences to the contrary, there's a habit of assuming that our physical body and our beliefs and other thoughts are what is most important, so much so that we think that everything that pops into our heads is important. We even use the argument, "That's what I think" to justify our position, as if thinking something makes it true. Since our most common thought or assumption is the assumption that "I am the body" or "I am my thoughts, feelings, and desires," this pointing to the falseness or incompleteness of those most basic beliefs is vitally important to loosening the grip of the ego.

However, in the absence of the experience of our true nature, there is this danger of the sense of self simply landing on a new belief in no self. The sense of self moves from a limited and painful identification with the mind's idea of who you are to a more open and freeing idea of emptiness and non-existence. While this may be a relief, it can eventually be just as limiting as the original ego identification. When our sense of self has identified with nothingness, emptiness, or no self, we can become stuck there. This is often reflected in a kind of defensiveness of this new identification: Anytime you are challenged, you deflect the criticism or conflict by retreating more fully into the idea of no self.

Or you turn the tables on those challenging you and try to convince them that they don't exist, therefore their concerns aren't valid. This new identification with no self can feel flat, dry, and detached. Life feels like it has no meaning or value. So what was once a helpful and freeing dissolving of limiting structures has become a new fossilized and limiting identity.

Because it is your essential identity or sense of self that moves into or identifies with the concept of emptiness or no self, it is a very convincing new identification. Whenever identity moves into an experience, it doesn't just experience it but actually becomes it to a degree. When your sense of self is firmly planted in the body and egoic mind, it feels like that is who you are. And when, instead of just experiencing emptiness, your identity or sense of self moves fully into emptiness or no self, it also is very convincingly felt as who you are. When you move so fully into identification with something that it no longer feels like an experience but who you really are, the experience becomes more global and convincing.

This is the power of identification to make an egoic thought and the false self, or ego, seem more real than it is. The power of identification can also make the dry emptiness and meaninglessness of no self seem more real. They are both illusions, but it is through identification that illusions are made to seem real. Being or consciousness is ultimately the one that is identifying, and when limitless eternal Being identifies to create illusion, it does a good job of it!

However, no matter how powerful the illusion of the egoic self or no self is when we are identified with it, identification is still simply a movement of thought followed by a movement of our sense of self into that thought. Since thought is always a temporary phenomenon, no identification is ever permanent. In fact, every identification only lasts as long as the thought triggering it. We become "stuck" in identification by repeating a lot of similar thoughts. The sense of an egoic self or no self are both created by a pattern of repeated thoughts that identity moves into.

Because this movement of thought is temporary, there is always, in every moment, the possibility of touching the deeper reality of our true nature. What is even more amazing is when, with repeated experiences of our true nature, our identity, or sense of self, moves into the realm of essential reality. Eventually it becomes obvious that Presence is actually who we are. When our identity moves into our true nature, there is no suffering and no dryness or emptiness. We simply are all of the peace, joy, and love in the universe.

There is nothing you can do to move your identity, or sense of self, into your true nature. Identity isn't something you do; it is what you are. However, the sense of identity follows your awareness, and since you are ultimately everything, it can and will identify with whatever is in your awareness. This is the danger of a teaching that doesn't point to or convey the existence of true nature. If something isn't even talked about or considered, it's much less likely that awareness will notice it and that identity will shift into it. This is why it's important to teach and explore all the qualities of Presence, such as joy, peace, and love, so that awareness begins to touch them and identity eventually shifts to the underlying truth of Being.

A subtle distinction needs to be made between your true identity and the sense of self you have in any moment. Your true identity has and always will be the infinite spaciousness of Being, including all forms, both physical and subtle, and all of the formless emptiness of pure space. But your sense of self is a flexible means for this limitless Being to experience itself from many different perspectives. By having this ability to move in and out of all kinds of experiences and appear to become them by identifying with them, Being gets to try on many different experiences or illusions, from the most contracted and limited to the most expanded and blissful. Without this capacity, Being would be a static existence of infinite potential that is never expressed. By moving its identity into and identifying with the myriad perspectives of limited experience, this potential becomes experienced in form and movement.

So while mis-identification is the root of all your "problems," it isn't and never has been a mistake. Being has very purposefully shifted its identity in and out of infinite apparent selves to try them all on for size. Being stuck in identification is itself an illusion, since all identification is temporary. Every expression of life is an expression of the right way to be, if the right way to be is simply to express our limitless capacity to experience identification and dis-identification, form and formlessness. The deepest, fullest experience of anything is to become it, and that is what Being has been up to all along.

The ultimate freedom is the discovery that it is fine to identify and dis-identify. True freedom demands no limits, not even limits against limitation. Since Being itself is completely free and cannot be harmed, it has been endlessly exploring every possibility of that freedom. This perspective will allow you to hold everything, even the spiritual journey, lightly. The goal is and always has been the journey itself. You can be curious about this whole process of identification with the ego, with no self, and with true nature simply for its own sake. It is a rich and mysterious world of perception and reality that we as consciousness inhabit. Why not taste it all? Life is and has always been this endless movement in and out of identification, in and out of forms and formlessness.

Finally, here is a short fairy tale about Being, which captures some of this freedom in a story:

Once upon no time, there was an infinite and eternal Being. Needless to say this was one big Being. Being infinite and eternal meant that no matter where or when it went, there it was. And of course, anything that big was made of empty space, as space is the only thing big enough to be that infinite.

While space is a wonderfully low maintenance thing to be, since it can't be harmed, this Being still had a problem: There was no one else. Since it was already everywhere and every-when, there was no place or time for anyone else. It was not a horrible problem, but still there was no one else to talk to, dance with, or play with.

What's an infinite Being to do? It can't really just create lesser beings inside of itself as that would not be very interesting to an infinite Being. For a truly infinite and eternal being to create little lesser beings to play with would be like you or me making dolls to play with as an adult. There's nothing wrong with that, but that's not very interesting after a while.

Then it had a great idea! Being infinite meant it also had infinite potential, so rather than create lesser beings, it decided to create more infinite beings. At first this would seem impossible since there is the question of where would you put another infinite Being? There already is no space left over once you have one infinite Being. But the great thing about space is that it is completely empty as long as it's pure space or pure potential, so two spaces can actually occupy the same space!

That was the solution! So Being created an infinite number of infinite space Beings just like itself. In a sense, Being cloned itself. Now, rather than having just a wind-up doll version of a Being to relate to, it had real, fully amazing infinite Beings like itself to relate to.

Even better, it quickly discovered that as long as one of the infinite space Beings stayed "home" as infinite space to hold the endless universes in place, then all of the rest were free to contract into all kinds of shapes and sizes. In fact, all a Being of infinite potential has to do to contract into a different shape or size is think about it, and voila it happens! That's the power of infinite potential!

Now not only could all these infinite Beings hang out as one very big space (which of course really meant hanging out as one Being, since two spaces in the same space are really still just one space), they could also play at contracting into all kinds of lesser expressions of their infinite potential.

Now why would they want to do that? Why would something infinite want to experience being less than its infinite self? Well remember these Beings are not only infinite, but also eternal, and eternity is a very long time! That means they all had a lot of time to kill. What does it matter if you spend a little time experiencing yourself as less than your complete potential, especially if you can do an entire eon standing on your head and still have all the time in the world?

And so Being, as many Beings, was now free to talk, dance, create, and play in all kinds of crazy wonderful ways because now there was someone else to talk, dance, create, and play with. Party time!!!

Ever since, it has been discovering all of the different things it can identify with and temporarily become and all of the truly strange and amazing things it can do once it has become less than itself. Infinite space can't really play soccer or be a super nova or fall in love or have its heart broken or create a new universe or fly a kite when it's expanded into its original nature as infinite space, but if it contracts into a form or expression of itself, then it can do all of that and more!

So that is what it's been up to ever since, and it's really just getting started, since it still has so much time on its hands; the rest of eternity is still a very long time. That is also why it's so amazing to relate to others: because it is never some lesser incomplete being across the table from you. It is always an infinite Being with infinite potential that *you are talking to or playing with. No wonder they are so convincing in their role as an apparent separate individual. It is really God playing that role. There are only Gods upon Gods upon Gods being everybody and everything and doing everything that is done! That is what we all are.*

Pretty clever solution if you want to have some fun, don't you think?

***

I am That.
You are That.
And that is that.

APPENDIX

Nirmala's Story

(Adapted from a talk given in Boulder, Colorado in 1999)

The important thing to remember is that this is just a story and that nothing I'm going to say now is at all necessary or relevant to knowing who you really are. There are a few exceptions to that, which I'll point out along the way.

About two years ago, I was busy attending naturopathic medical school and, I thought, happily married. Then out of the blue, at least from my perspective, my wife told me she was leaving me for another man. The intensity of the feelings that surfaced was amazing. I was aware of feeling equal and opposite feelings: intense feelings of both grief over the loss and relief from being released from the struggle of making a relationship work. Amidst overwhelming, paralyzing fear was intense excitement over all the new possibilities created by the space that had opened up in my life.

Upon reflection, I realized that this had always been the case, that in every experience in my life I've always had equal and opposite feelings. That's just the nature of feelings—they're always present in opposite pairs. For instance, with naturopathic medical school, I was both enjoying and resisting every minute of it. The problem was that these opposing feelings were so intense in the days and weeks after my wife left me. It felt like I wasn't a big enough container for that much fear and that much excitement, that much sadness and that much relief. I felt like I was being torn apart or stretched, and I couldn't contain all the disparate emotions.

Then, by luck or by grace, I heard about something called The Sedona Method, which is a technique for releasing emotions or, alternatively, for just allowing them to be there with no need to release them. It's based on the idea that there is no need to repress emotions or express them—you just let them be, or just let them go. It was so obviously appropriate for me that I had to check it out. I called up Hale Dwoskin of the Sedona Institute and ordered the tapes that taught the method. I had a week off and just sat down and went through the tapes.

The Sedona Method starts off with letting go of all the uncomfortable emotions. Then what is revealed are the more positive emotions, which it also suggests you let go of. One day I was practicing this technique, and I had a moment when I followed it all the way—I just let go of everything, all the painful emotions and all the peace, happiness, and joy. I just let it all go, and there was an incredible silence that I'd never experienced before. It happened when I was out for a walk, and suddenly I was so present to everything—the trees, the sidewalk, and the sky. I was so moved by this experience of silence that I immediately turned around, went home, called Hale, and asked him if I could come to an advanced training, even though I was just a beginner. He said, "Sure, come on." I signed up thinking I'd get more of this wonderful technique, which I saw as a profound form of stress relief.

What I didn't know at the time was that The Sedona Method had been developed by a man named Lester Levinson as a tool for awakening to one's true nature as limitless Freedom, and there was a whole community of people who had spent ten, fifteen, or even twenty years using this method in the effort to become awakened, or free. Finally, one of them (other than Lester, who had died a few years earlier) had "made it." Her name was Pamela, and she was co-teaching the advanced Sedona Method course. When I showed up at the course, I saw a room full of forty or so people, all desperate to awaken. I was resistant at first, but I had to admit there was something about Pamela that was undeniably attractive. She had a presence of pure happiness and a real sense of Freedom.

It also happened that Pamela had made arrangements for a spiritual teacher named Neelam to come to town to give satsang. At the time, I didn't even know what "satsang" meant. Every day, we practiced The Sedona Method, and every night we went to satsang with Neelam. This undeniable sense of Freedom that I had felt in Pamela was even more present in Neelam. Even though my mind couldn't grasp it, I couldn't let it go; I couldn't forget about it. I looked around the room at everyone else who had come, and I saw them really suffering over their desire to awaken. It was almost palpable; they wanted it so badly. However, I found myself holding back. I wanted to be like Pamela and Neelam, but I definitely didn't want to be like everybody else. It felt safer just to pretend that I didn't want it.

In one of the classes, Hale presented a chart of wants, and the last want, the most fundamental desire, was the desire for Freedom. He spoke about the desire for Freedom as the desire that burns away all the other desires, which paradoxically, you also must let go of. That night, in my room all alone, I had this great idea— why not take a short cut and just let go of the desire for Freedom? I thought, "I'll start at the end, at the last step. I'll let go of the desire for Freedom, and then I will be Free." But a troubling doubt appeared: "What if I'm fooling myself? This short cut could be like cheating. I'd better ask Hale about it tomorrow."

Then I remembered that Hale rarely answers questions; he just does The Sedona Method until you get the answer from within. So I figured I must already know the answer, and I just got very quiet and asked inside, "Can I use this shortcut to become free?" The answer that came was: "It's not up to you. There's nothing you can do to become free." At that moment I knew this was true beyond a shadow of a doubt—there was absolutely nothing "I" could do about it. It was simply not up to me.

The fact that I couldn't do anything about it was a completely devastating realization because, in that exact same moment, I also realized that I wanted Freedom more than I'd ever wanted anything in my life. And I burst into tears—not just sobbing, but wailing for hours because I realized there was absolutely nothing I could do about this thing that I wanted more than life itself. And yet, after being in the presence of Pamela and Neelam, I just couldn't let it go. I had this sense there was surgery going on in my chest, like it had been ripped open. This is one of those important elements to the story. I could just stop the story here because once I had admitted I wanted this Freedom more than anything else, even though I absolutely knew there was nothing I could do about it, there was no turning back to my old life.

A few weeks later I was at a satsang retreat with Neelam, and at one point she moved into the center of my heart. I suddenly knew that whatever it took, I was going to be with Neelam. She was a master at completely bypassing my mind. I would formulate these nice, neat questions, and she would lovingly pop them like a balloon. There's no way I could get around her, through her, or past her with my mind.

So, I gave my share in our house to my wife and quit medical school. These are the irrelevant parts, by the way. You don't need to have a spouse leave you. You don't have to give away your house, drop out of school, quit your job—whatever. But I did all that to follow Neelam through Europe and on to India. I had never had a strong desire to go to India with all its poverty, disease, and other challenges. And I had even less desire to go, now that I was going. Going to India had nothing to do with wanting to go to India; that was just where Neelam was going to be.

The next relevant point in this story came during a satsang in England, on the way to India. I can't remember exactly what Neelam said, but in that same way that I'd known there was nothing I could do to get Freedom, I also knew that there was nothing that I had to fix about myself first to become Free. There was truly nothing I had to change or improve. Trying to fix myself, make myself perfect, had been a lifelong task and a huge burden because it was so obvious that it was hopeless. I had participated in endless workshops, trainings, and self-improvement techniques— even The Sedona Method. They were all attempts to become better. Finally, from what Neelam said, I got it that none of that was necessary. So not only was there nothing I could do to become Free, but fortunately I now recognized that neither was there anything I had to do to become Free.

From that point, I just got happier and happier. Even awakening and Freedom no longer mattered. I was perfectly happy the way things were. For example, I used to run the sound equipment for Neelam, and one day, fifteen minutes into satsang the whole system stopped working. I was pushing buttons and turning knobs, and it just wouldn't work. Meanwhile, I was just getting happier and happier—"It's wonderful, the system's not working!" It's just that it really didn't matter anymore—even this whole notion of awakening or Freedom. I was ready to spend the rest of my life going to satsang with Neelam, running the sound equipment. This was the letting go of even the desire for Freedom that Hale had spoken about.

Eventually, we went on to India and ended up in Rishikesh at an ashram called Phool Chatti in the jungle on the banks of the Ganges. There we spent our days in satsang with Neelam and our nights singing devotional songs.

Whenever I wasn't in satsang, I sat by the river, especially late at night after everyone had gone to sleep. I would sit about ten feet from the edge of the Ganges along this stretch of ten-foot tall rapids. The river was an incredible roaring presence of rushing white water.

One night as I was sitting there under the full moon, I recognized that the rock I was leaning on was me—"Oh yeah, this is me; this rock is inside of me." Once I realized that about that rock, I saw the same was true of all the rocks in the huge field of boulders along the river's edge. Then since the rocks were so obviously "me," the river was obviously "me" too, not just this stretch of the river, but the entire Ganges from one end of India to the other. Very quickly, I saw that not just the river, but the whole continent was "me." It struck me as obvious that it was all inside "me"—and then it was the whole world, and the whole solar system, the entire galaxy and universe. This kept going until the mind couldn't keep up. There was no longer any possibility of my mind containing all of this endless space, and yet it was all "me" in the same way that one of my limbs was "me."

Then there was a wonderful moment when "me" included not only infinity in terms of space, but "popped" to also include all time. It was obviously who I had always been, and it included all the past and all the future. Then I laughed and laughed and rolled around in the gravel because it was suddenly so silly that I had imagined myself to have suffered. I had always been so free that I was even free to have this illusion of not being free. That's how complete the Freedom is. So I just laughed and laughed.

I sometimes call this experience a non-awakening because what I realized in that moment is that all there is and ever has been is Awakeness. There's no need for awakening in Awakeness itself. All of life is just the play of this that has always been fully awake.

I would like to emphasize again that the specifics of this experience aren't important. This Awakeness/Consciousness doesn't even make a snowflake the same way twice, so it is reasonable to assume that it wouldn't have an awakening experience the same way twice. What is important is the transformation of perspective that the experience allows. The shift in perspective to knowing that you are already free doesn't depend on having any particular experience.

Since that time, there has been a simple desire to share the perspective of Freedom. I began doing this in informal conversations with friends and then through giving satsang after being invited to.

> time on my hands
> can I wash them clean
> send the past down the drain
> scrub away the future
> leaving nice pink rosy fingers of now
> touching everything within easy reach
> and yet grasping only momentarily
> to express my depth of gratitude
> for the warmth in every touch
> then releasing it forever
> before a memory
> sticks to my skin

and calls me back to the sink
for another washing

time out of my hands
I can only touch
but can never hold more than a single breath
until it too goes
leaving only another now
no scrubbing needed

Interview with Nirmala

(From a radio interview by Andrea Young in July, 2000)

Andrea (A): Can you tell us a little bit about yourself? Do you consider yourself in the spiritual tradition of Advaita Vedanta?

Nirmala (N): I don't label myself as anything. It's simpler that way; it's truer. There are no certifying boards for spiritual teachers, so I don't claim to be anything.

(A): Is it that you consider yourself a spiritual teacher?

(N): I finally figured that I had to call myself something, so I settled on "spiritual teacher," as the least distorting description. It's simpler than saying, "Ahhh" and not having an answer whenever someone asks what you do.

(A): For those listeners out there who know this interview has something to do with spirituality, what would you tell them is most important?

(N): It's actually a very simple message: The peace and love and happiness that we've all been seeking is always already present. It's always here right now, before, during, and after any seeking you do. And that's wonderful news because you can just rest, you can just stop, you can just be in this Truth. And it's, at the same time, really bad news if you're a spiritual seeker because when you find out that what you've been seeking is already present, you're out of a job.

The job description for the ego now is to do nothing, and that's not such good news for the ego. The ego likes the job of spiritual seeker. It gives it something to do. It adds a lot of beauty and drama and intensity to life, to be seeking for the truth. Then to find out that it's already here—that it's present in every moment—can be a shock. But it's also really wonderful news because then you finally get to rest; you finally get to just be in the Truth that you are, which is this Love.

Actually it's more accurate to say that the source of peace, the source of love, the source of happiness is always present because it sometimes appears with the quality of peace, and in another moment, it appears with the quality of love. Strangely enough, the source that is the source of peace, love, wisdom, and happiness is actually the source of everything. That makes the spiritual seeker's job even smaller because you don't even have to weed out the peace from everything else that's present. It's all coming from the same source, so there's no need to get rid of anything for the source of peace to be recognized.

(A): Would you say that your message is only for spiritual seekers then?

(N): No, actually the message is for everyone, and in fact it's a great blessing if you're lucky enough to skip the stage of being a spiritual seeker. You don't have to go through quite as much identification with that kind of struggle. If you're lucky enough to hear this Truth before you've gone looking for it, it can save you a lot of trouble.

(A): And isn't this Truth really just Being, just Beingness? Isn't it like, sort of a joke?

(N): Yes, it is a wonderful joke because this Beingness is always present, even before you knew to look for it. The joke is that Beingness is very ordinary; the joke is that it's the most natural thing about all of us, about every experience. The source of all has no qualities, and yet all of these qualities of peace and quiet and stillness and loving embrace all come out of it. But the joke is that it is also present in very ordinary moments. It is also that which listens to the news every night on TV. It is also that which brushes your teeth every morning. It is also that which sometimes gets irritated at your neighbor. It is also that which takes the dog out for a walk. It is present in all of those different experiences, all of the different emotions, all of the different thoughts. They are all occurring in and coming from this Presence, this empty kind of Presence that is the source of everything.

(A): Do you see, as other teachers do, that this is quite an extraordinary time, in that very ordinary people are waking up?

(N): Yes there seems to be a greater possibility today of recognizing this Truth. Recognizing this very ordinary and yet also extraordinary Presence is easier now, and I have no idea why that is; it's just an observation. It is happening to people who've been long-time spiritual seekers, and it's happening to people who don't have a spiritual bone in their body.

(A): Have you always been a spiritual seeker?

(N): I went through a period, in my teens, when I was deeply involved with spiritual seeking; and then it seemed like I needed to go out and live in the world and find out what that was all about. I couldn't take a short cut. I first had to try to make it in the real world of careers and marriage and owning a house. It was only when I had been successful in a material sense and had that success fall apart that I found myself looking for a deeper truth again— something that was more satisfying. I found that there wasn't real happiness in the surface of things and that I had to go to the source for that.

(A): And was there a path that took you there? Obviously there was.

(N): You know, the great thing about my teacher is that she wouldn't teach me anything: She wouldn't give me a path. She wouldn't give me anything to do. Anytime I tried to turn her words into a way of understanding, a way of grasping onto this Truth and containing it in an understanding, she would pull the rug out from underneath me. And yet, there was something about her that was undeniable. There was a Presence, an atmosphere around her that was irresistible. I dropped everything in my life to be in her presence. But there was also nothing there for me: There was no understanding, no great teaching or path to follow, no great explanation of everything. Instead, it was up to me to let go of all of that and find that Presence in myself. And there is no "how." The closest thing to how is to do nothing, be quiet, rest. The mind doesn't like that because it doesn't get any credit that way.

(A): And when you say "rest," obviously you're not talking about sitting down on the sofa and not moving for a period of time. Do you mean resting the mind?

(N): I mean resting from the struggle to find the Truth, resting from doing anything to improve yourself or your experiences or your emotional state. Obviously, you still get up in the morning and eat breakfast and go about your day. It's a surrendering of all of the effort to make this Love and Peace that is already present be present. When you drop the effort, then the underlying Truth that it is already here becomes obvious.

(A): Do you mean dropping the effort, whether it be in creating happiness or in being happy or sad or whatever the emotions or whatever's going on?

(N): It is so wonderfully simple: It's already here. There's nothing for you to do. When you realize this, then there is the possibility of just looking in your present moment experience and finding what's already present here and now. I would also add that this Truth, this place of peace and quiet, can often seem very quiet and small. So at first, you may only have a very small recognition in your Heart that there is Love already present, there is peace, there is acceptance of the way things are. This recognition may be very small and therefore seem insignificant. But if you give that little sliver of peace that's present right now your full attention, you may find that—even though it is very quiet, very simple, and very ordinary— this Peace is actually very big, very vast and that it is much bigger than your so-called problems or your sadness or fear or anger. It turns out that this quiet, simple Truth is much bigger than what you first think. The invitation is to give this peaceful, aware Presence all of your attention, to trust the one thing you can trust, which is your own Heart, your own recognition of Truth.

(A): Well, I know that some of the listeners must have the same questions I have, and I'm sitting here thinking, yes, but how are we going to get world peace and how are we going to make goodness happen in the world, because it almost sounds to me like not doing, nondoing.

(N): In the teaching I do, which is called satsang, I'm often pointing to the half of the truth that people are overlooking. This quiet, peaceful place of Beingness is the place we lose track of when we're so involved in doing in the world and making the world a better place and making our lives better. So the pointing is to this overlooked half of the truth. But that still is only half of the story.

Once there's been a recognition of this deeper, more all-inclusive Truth, it would be a big mistake to hide from the world in this peaceful Beingness. One of the potential pitfalls is a tendency to hide out there, to think, "Now I've got peace, so I can't be bothered with the rest of the world." If you do try to hide, what you've done is formed a new ego, a new spiritual ego as someone who has become enlightened or awakened. You've just shifted your identity to an equally limited part of yourself.

Beyond that, is the opportunity to bring this realization into action in the world and to find out what this peaceful, loving Presence is capable of. For this, the most important question is: "Where is this action coming from?" If you're trying to save the world out of a place of personal interest and identity, it may look like you're doing good work; but if you scratch beneath the surface, what it's really about is making you look better and satisfying your personal desires and needs.

However, something profound can happen when you embrace the whole truth. Not only are you willing to recognize the perfection that is always present, even before the world has been fixed, you are also willing to look your own life, your own actions, and the world straight in the eye and see what is in alignment with this bigger view, and what needs to be changed to be in alignment. Then the changes can come from a place of loving acceptance instead of a place of painful resistance. When change comes from a place of loving acceptance, it is more often based on a clear and true seeing of what is needed. When change comes from a place of painful resistance, it is often based on personal needs or desires, and it isn't as wise.

In the whole truth, what is missing is the sense that it's all about me. That is the other reason why it isn't good news for the ego to find out that peace, love, and happiness are already here. Because along with the job of seeker, what also goes is the sense of the Truth having anything to do with you. There's nothing personal about this Truth; it is very impersonal. And yet, when you are aligned with the Truth, you are completely at ease in the world and do whatever needs to be done.

I read a quote recently where another teacher said he doesn't understand what all the big fuss is about enlightenment because, to him, the only value of enlightenment is if it allows there to be more love in the world. Enlightenment for enlightenment's sake is just a way to get your own needs met. So unless that realization is put in service to the Truth, and this peaceful, loving Presence is put into expression in the world, then what's the point—what's the difference whether someone is enlightened or not?

(A): Well, I guess I would ask you that question, what is the point?

(N): The ultimate truth is always one step ahead.... so it's always a mystery. When we see very loving actions coming out of someone who has had a profound spiritual experience, we often think that all we have to do is act like them, and then we'll have profound spiritual experiences too. So we act like Mother Theresa or we act like an Indian saint. But where are these actions coming from, what are they in service to? If they are in service to an idea of yourself as a spiritual and, therefore, special person, then those actions will get distorted by your needs. But if they are coming from Love, which isn't personal, which isn't yours in any sense, then they have a freshness and unpredictable spontaneity to them. One of the qualities of this Presence is that it is very fresh, very unexpected. My teacher was a master at totally surprising me. Whatever I thought she would do, she would do something so completely different and unexpected that I would be left breathless in astonishment.

(A): Who is your teacher?

(N): My teacher's name is Neelam. She spent time in India with Papaji, who was her teacher.

(A): What does your name mean, and where does it come from?

(N): I got my name from Neelam. It's a Sanskrit word that means "pure." A friend of mine gave me a bar of soap from India. Just like Ivory soap says "pure" on the box, this soap said "nirmala."

(A): What part of your work brings you the most satisfaction?

(N): What is amazing to me is how much satisfaction I find in everything nowadays. There is a great sense of joy when someone is getting this simple message, and there is a great sense of joy and wonder when someone is struggling. And there is a great sense of joy when I'm resting in what is, and there is also a great sense of joy and wonder when I get caught again in suffering, by trying to make my life better or do it better.

(A): Would you say something about how one might directly experience something one has fought all one's life?

(N): Do you mean a part of your life that's not fulfilling or giving you trouble?

(A): Yes, in the sense of something that you push away.

(N): The simplest thing is to start with whatever is, whatever is present. If it's really true that the source of everything you've been seeking is already here, then the obvious thing is to start with whatever is here. So if what is, is that you are resisting or pushing away something, then you get curious about that. Find out what the experience of resistance is. Who or what is resisting? What is that really like?

One quality of this Truth, this mystery that we are, is awareness—it has consciousness. It's hearing this voice right now and feeling the sensations of the body in this moment. So awareness is present, right now. This is a good quality to start with to understand this mystery because it is always present. Even if you're in great suffering, in great struggle and resisting life with all your might, there's also awareness of the resistance. This may not seem like that big a deal, but the invitation is to notice what is aware of the resistance? What is this very ordinary quality of experience we call awareness that is always present?

Without doing anything to the resistance or to the problem causing it, just notice that there's also awareness present, and get curious about that. Then, some wonderful questions can be asked:

What is Awareness's perspective on this problem? And what is Awareness's perspective on your resistance to it? The funny thing is, Awareness doesn't have a problem with anything, not even with your resisting your problems. So when you ask that question, when you look out from a place of just Awareness, you can't find problems anymore. All of the same elements are still present in your life, but Awareness itself has no problem with any of them.

(A): In being enlightened, does it mean that you always recognize this Awareness or that you've had some big wake-up call?

(N): Like everything else in life, no two people experience any aspect of life the same way. The same thing is true of this experience that the word enlightenment points to: There is no formula for it. There are people for whom it's a big, explosive experience that completely obliterates any suffering or struggle or resistance. And there are others who very gradually, almost imperceptibly, have moved into a place where they are recognizing and living out of more and more of the Truth. I have friends who don't consider themselves enlightened because they never had a big experience, while it's obvious to everyone around them that they are living out of an enlightened perspective.

Because of all these different experiences, any formula you put on this very mysterious thing we call enlightenment or awakening is going to unnecessarily limit it.

(A): Do you still struggle?

(N): I was telling a friend over lunch today that the difference is that I can't keep up the struggling for very long. Now when I start to struggle with what is happening or go to battle with reality, the experience is similar to putting on a pair of underwear that's about five sizes too small. In the past, I would pull that underwear on anyway because it was *my* underwear, dammit, and I was determined to wear it until I wore it out. Now it's more like I get the underwear half way up and say, "Nah, it's not worth it." So I can't say that there is never a movement to resist, but when resistance occurs, it's very difficult to sustain it because there's such a recognition of the contrast between the suffering and this place of peace. The contrast is so obvious that there's less tendency to keep going, to fight and struggle all the way into the too- tight underwear of a so-called problem.

(A): Do you feel that you are a channel for some energy or entity?

(N): I don't feel that I am anything. So all there really is, is this energy, this Presence. Another way of saying the same thing is that everything is a channel for this energy; everything is an expression of this Presence. The Presence itself has no preferences. There is no better expression of this Presence. It is all perfect; it is all beautiful just the way it is.

(A): And would you say your realization is still deepening?

(N): Endlessly, endlessly. I feel like I've barely scratched the surface.

(A): And if there's one thing you would say to our listeners today to assist them in seeking Truth, what would that be?

(N): Simply check beneath your shoulders. It's not that the truth is located anywhere physically in your body, but somehow in including the knowing that comes from beneath your shoulders, you automatically include more of your Being than just your mind. It's not that the mind is wrong or a mistake, but when you include more of your Being, there is more of a recognition of the whole truth. Especially include your Heart when you look for the truth of your experience. When you include the Heart in finding out what is true, you include this impersonal, yet wise and clear Presence that is always here. What is it that your Heart knows in this moment already? What is it that is already present in your Heart?

ABOUT THE AUTHOR

After a lifetime of spiritual seeking, Nirmala met his teacher, Neelam, a devotee of H.W.L. Poonja (Papaji). She convinced Nirmala that seeking wasn't necessary; and after experiencing a profound spiritual awakening in India, he began offering satsang and Nondual Spiritual Mentoring with Neelam's blessing. This tradition of spiritual wisdom has been most profoundly disseminated by Ramana Maharshi, a revered Indian saint, who was Papaji's teacher. Nirmala's perspective was also profoundly expanded by his friend and teacher, Adyashanti.

Nirmala offers a unique vision and a gentle, compassionate approach, which adds to this rich tradition of inquiry into the truth of Being. He is also the author of *Living from the Heart*, *Nothing Personal: Seeing Beyond the Illusion of a Separate Self*, and *Gifts with No Giver*. He has been offering satsang throughout the United States and Canada since 1998. He lives in Sedona, Arizona with his wife, Gina Lake.

Watch videos of Nirmala and download free book excerpts and ebooks at:

www.endless-satsang.com

Nondual Spiritual Mentoring

Nondual Spiritual Mentoring with Nirmala is available to support you in giving attention and awareness to the more subtle and yet more satisfying inner dimensions of your being. Whether it is for a single spiritual mentoring session or for ongoing one-to-one spiritual guidance, this is an opportunity for you to more completely orient your life toward the true source of peace, joy, and happiness, especially if there is not ongoing satsang or other support available in your location. As a spiritual teacher and spiritual mentor, Nirmala has worked with thousands of individuals and groups around the world to bring people into a direct experience of the spiritual truth of oneness beyond the illusion of separation. He especially enjoys working with individuals in one-to-one sessions because of the greater depth and intimacy possible.

Mentoring sessions with Nirmala are an opportunity for open-ended inquiry. In your session, you can ask any questions, raise any concerns that are meaningful to you, or simply explore your present moment experience, which is a doorway into a deeper reality. Regular weekly, biweekly, or monthly mentoring sessions can be especially transformative. These mentoring sessions are offered in person or over the phone and typically last an hour. If you live outside the US or Canada, you must initiate the call.

To contact Nirmala, please visit www.endless-satsang.com.

Made in the USA
Lexington, KY
17 October 2010